# REVISE PEARSON EDEXCEL GCSE (9–1)

# History

## WEIMAR AND NAZI GERMANY, 1918–39

# PRACTICE PAPER Plus⁺

T0345702

Series Consultant: Harry Smith

Author: Sally Clifford

This Practice Paper is designed to complement your revision and to help you prepare for the exam. It does not include all the content and skills you need for the complete course and has been written to help you practise what you have learned. It may not be representative of a real exam paper. Remember that the official Pearson specification and associated assessment guidance materials are the only authoritative source of information and you should always refer to them for definitive guidance.

For further information, go to: quals.pearson.com/GCSEHistory

Published by Pearson Education Limited, 80 Strand, London, WC2R 0RL.

www.pearsonschoolsandfecolleges.co.uk

Copies of official specifications for all Pearson qualifications may be found on the website: qualifications.pearson.com

Text and illustrations © Pearson Education Ltd 2020

Produced, typeset and illustrated by QBS Learning

Cover illustration by Eoin Coveney

The right of Sally Clifford to be identified as author of this work has been asserted by her in accordance with the Copyright, Designs and Patents Act 1988.

First published 2020

23 22 21 20

10 9 8 7 6 5 4 3 2 1

**British Library Cataloguing in Publication Data**

A catalogue record for this book is available from the British Library

ISBN 978 1 292 31013 8

**Copyright notice**

All rights reserved. No part of this publication may be reproduced in any form or by any means (including photocopying or storing it in any medium by electronic means and whether or not transiently or incidentally to some other use of this publication) without the written permission of the copyright owner, except in accordance with the provisions of the Copyright, Designs and Patents Act 1988 or under the terms of a licence issued by the Copyright Licensing Agency, 5th Floor, Shackleton House, Hay's Galleria, 4 Battle Bridge Lane, London, SE1 2HX (www.cla.co.uk). Applications for the copyright owner's written permission should be addressed to the publisher.

Printed in Italy by L.E.G.O. SpA

**Acknowledgements**

Content written by Ben Armstrong is included.

**Text Credits:**

**P11 Randall Bytwerk and Achim Gercke:** Extract from Gercke, Achim, 'Solving the Jewish Question' (translation), © Randall Bytwerk. Retrieved from https://research.calvin.edu/german-propaganda-archive/gercke.htm. Accessed: 04 Sept 2019, **P14 Holocaust Memorial Day Trust:** Adapted from 'Nazi Persecution 1933 – 1945', https://www.hmd.org.uk/learn-about-the-holocaust-and-genocides/nazi-persecution/. © Holocaust Memorial Day Trust; **P14 Yad Vashem:** Adapted text from '1938 – The Fateful Year' https://www.yadvashem.org/holocaust/about/nazi-germany-1933-39/1938.html. Accessed: 10 November 2019 © Yad Vashem, 2019; **P44 Adolf Hitler:** Extract from speech 17 April 1923. Published in 'Aspects of Western Civilization, Volume II' Perry Rogers, ed.; Prentice Hall (2000) 978-0130489685; **P57 Macmillan Publishers Ltd.:** Diesel, Eugen. Extract from 'Germany and the Germans', (London 1931), translated from Die deutsche Wandlung das Bild eines Volks (Stuttgart, 1931), p255–6; **P58 Kershaw, Ian.** Extract from 'Hitler, 1889–1936: Hubris'. Penguin Press History, 1999. 9780140288988. p409; **P58 Pelican books:** Bullock, Alan. Extract from 'Hitler, A Study in Tyranny'. Pelican Editions, 1962, p151; **P59 Adolf Hitler:** Extract from speech 17 April 1923. Published in 'Aspects of Western Civilization, Volume II' Perry Rogers, ed.; Prentice Hall (2000) 978-0130489685.

**Image Credits:**

**123RF:** Johan2011 27; **Alamy Stock Photo:** Chronicle 57. **Getty Images:** Galerie Bilderwelt/Hulton Archive 19, **United States Holocaust Memorial Museum, Washington/Wikimedia Foundation:** Kennzeichen für Schutzhäftlinge in den Konzentrationslagern.jpg, circa 1932. Public domain image shared for the public domain with thanks to the United States Holocaust Memorial Museum, who posted the picture first 11.

**Notes from the publisher**

1. While the publishers have made every attempt to ensure that advice on the qualification and its assessment is accurate, the official specification and associated assessment guidance materials are the only authoritative source of information and should always be referred to for definitive guidance. Pearson examiners have not contributed to any sections in this resource relevant to examination papers for which they have responsibility.

2. Pearson has robust editorial processes, including answer and fact checks, to ensure the accuracy of the content in this publication, and every effort is made to ensure this publication is free of errors. We are, however, only human, and occasionally errors do occur. Pearson is not liable for any misunderstandings that arise as a result of errors in this publication, but it is our priority to ensure that the content is accurate. If you spot an error, please do contact us at resourcescorrections@pearson.com so we can make sure it is corrected.

# Contents

## About this book

This book is designed to help you prepare for your Pearson Edexcel GCSE (9–1) History Weimar and Nazi Germany, 1918–39 exam. It focuses on the skills you will need to answer the exam questions successfully.

> You could work through the book in order. Alternatively, you could go straight to the section you want to focus on.

### ❶ Knowledge booster

✓ Get started with these quick, warm-up activities

✓ Recap what you already know about the topic

✓ Find out what you need to revise in more detail

✓ Use the links to the Revise Pearson Edexcel GCSE (9–1) History Revision Guide and Workbook to find more revision support

### ❷ Exam skills

✓ Get useful tips and guidance on how the exam works and what you need to do

✓ Understand how each question type works

✓ See how to write a successful answer with the 'steps to success' skills builders

✓ Learn how to avoid common mistakes

**This Practice Paper Plus book**

### ❸ Practice paper

✓ Write straight into this book

✓ Have a go at a full practice paper on this topic

✓ Use the hints and reminders in the margins to stay focused on what you need to do to answer each question successfully

✓ Tackle the paper under exam conditions by covering up the guidance in the margins

### ❹ Practice paper answers

✓ Read the mark schemes and notes to find out what a successful answer would include

✓ See full example answers to each question

✓ Look at the annotations and comments to understand what makes each answer successful

✓ Get ideas about how to improve your own responses in the exam

# The Weimar Republic, 1918–29

This key topic is about the Weimar Republic in the years 1918–29. It includes the origins of the Republic, the early challenges it faced, its economic recovery and how society changed.

**The legacy of the First World War and setting up the Weimar Republic**

1 Which of these was the main reason for the Kaiser's abdication in 1918? Tick (✓) the correct answer.

   **A.** The army refused to support him ☐    **C.** Ministers did not support him ☐

   **B.** He was worried by the strikes and riots ☐    **D.** He was blamed for the armistice terms ☐

2 Complete the table below. Add **one** more example to each column.

| Strengths of the Weimar constitution | Weaknesses of the Weimar constitution |
|---|---|
| • Proportional representation meant small parties were represented. | • Proportional representation often led to weak coalition governments. |

**Early challenges to the Weimar Republic, 1919–23**

3 Give **two** reasons why the Weimar Republic was unpopular.

   • ............................................................................................................................

   • ............................................................................................................................

4 Decide whether the descriptions below are about the Spartacists (S) or the Freikorps (F).

   **A.** Members of left-wing Independent Socialist Party ☐    **D.** Backed by Soviet Union ☐

   **B.** 250 000 ex-soldiers ☐    **E.** Attempted Kapp Putsch in 1920 ☐

   **C.** Right wing ☐    **F.** Took over news and telegraph bureau in 1919 ☐

**The challenges of 1923**

5 Fill in the gaps to complete this summary of the crisis in 1923.

Reparations payments damaged the German ........................................... . In 1922, the Weimar

government could not pay reparations and asked for more time. In ..........................................,

France invaded the ........................................... to take goods and raw materials instead.

German workers went on ........................................... . This was a disaster for the economy. The

government ........................................... more money to try to solve the problem but the value of

the mark kept dropping until it became worthless. This is called ........................................... .

# The Weimar Republic, 1918–29

**Reasons for economic recovery, 1924–29**

6  Complete the middle boxes in this flowchart about the recovery of the German economy.

> Stresemann sets up the Rentenmark, more secure, ends hyperinflation.

> Dawes Plan, 1924, ...

> Young Plan, ...

> Secure currency and US loans gave Germany longer to pay, government could reduce taxes, increase confidence, economy improves.

**Stresemann's achievements**

7  Draw lines to match the agreement on the left with the foreign policy on the right.

| | |
|---|---|
| **A.** Locarno Treaty | **i.** Germany initially excluded, set up in 1920. |
| **B.** Kellogg-Briand Pact | **ii.** Agreement between Germany, Britain, France, Italy and Belgium, including demilitarisation of Rhineland. |
| **C.** League of Nations | **iii.** Agreement between 62 nations to avoid war. |

8  Give **one** reason why Stresemann's achievements abroad were a success for Germany.

..............................................................................................................................................

**Changes in society**

9  Decide which statements are true and which are false. Circle your answers.

|   |   |   |   |
|---|---|---|---|
| **A.** | The house-building programme ended the housing shortage. | True | False |
| **B.** | A new unemployment insurance protected people who lost their jobs. | True | False |
| **C.** | High-status jobs became more available to women. | True | False |
| **D.** | New art movements like Expressionism began to flourish. | True | False |
| **E.** | Strict government controls meant that German cinema was very traditional. | True | False |
| **F.** | German architecture was very modern and innovative. | True | False |

**Revision Guide**

How did you do? Go to pages 1–9 of the Revision Guide to remind yourself of any points you aren't sure about, and for more about this key topic.

# Hitler's rise, 1919–33

This key topic is about Hitler's rise to power in the years 1919–33. It includes the early development of the Nazi Party, the Munich Putsch, changes in support for the Nazis and how Hitler became Chancellor.

**Hitler's early career and the growth of the Nazi Party**

1  (a)  Why did Hitler become a German nationalist?

.......................................................................................................................................

(b)  What did Hitler help to write in 1920?

.......................................................................................................................................

(c)  In what year did Hitler become the leader of the Nazi Party? .............................................

2  Define the term **Sturmabteilung**.

.......................................................................................................................................

.......................................................................................................................................

**The Munich Putsch, November 1923**

3  Which **two** of these were **long-term** reasons for the Munich Putsch? Tick (✓) the correct answers.

A.  Hyperinflation ☐            C.  Anger about reparations ☐

B.  'Stab in the back' ☐          D.  Hitler thought it was the right time ☐

4  Complete the table below about the consequences of the Munich Putsch for Hitler. Add **one** more example to each column.

| Negative consequences | Positive consequences |
|---|---|
| • Hitler was sent to prison. | • While he was in prison, he wrote *Mein Kampf*, which spread his ideas. |

**Party reorganisation**

5  Give **two** factors that led to the reorganisation of the Nazi Party.

•  .............................................................................................................................

•  .............................................................................................................................

6  Name the conference at which Hitler's control of the Nazi Party became clear.

.......................................................................................................................................

# Hitler's rise, 1919–33

**Rising unemployment: causes and impact**

7 Complete the middle boxes in this flowchart about unemployment in Germany, 1929–32.

After the 1929 Wall Street Crash, the USA stopped lending money to Germany and demanded all loans be repaid.

Government had no money, so ...

Businesses had to ...

Millions of job losses meant that ...

Impact of unemployment: support for the Nazis and the communists increases.

---

**Reasons for growth in support for Nazi Party, 1929–32**

8 Give **two** reasons for growth in support for the Nazi Party.

- ........................................................................................................................................
- ........................................................................................................................................

---

**Political developments in 1932**

9 Put these events in order. Write numbers in the boxes, from the earliest (1) to the latest (7).

- [ ] **A.** A coalition between the Nazis and other right-wingers takes power.
- [ ] **B.** Hindenburg elected as President, but Hitler increases share of the vote.
- [ ] **C.** Brüning resigns due to unpopularity.
- [ ] **D.** Von Papen persuades Hindenburg to appoint Hitler as Chancellor.
- [ ] **E.** Hitler demands that he is made Chancellor. Hindenburg refuses.
- [ ] **F.** Von Schleicher announces that he wants to lead a military dictatorship.
- [ ] **G.** Von Papen is forced out of office in favour of von Schleicher.

---

**Revision Guide**

How did you do? Go to pages 10–13 of the Revision Guide to remind yourself of any points you aren't sure about, and for more about this key topic.

# Nazi dictatorship, 1933–39

This key topic is about Nazi control and dictatorship in the years 1933–39. It includes the creation of the dictatorship, the police state, Nazi control, and support and opposition for the Nazi regime.

---

**The Reichstag Fire and the Enabling Act, 1933**

1 Who did Hitler blame for the Reichstag Fire? ...........................................

2 Which **three** of these were ways that the Enabling Act helped Hitler get rid of opposition? Tick (✓) the correct answers.

   **A.** Trade unions were banned    ☐     **C.** The constitution was scrapped    ☐

   **B.** Other political parties were banned    ☐     **D.** Hitler could pass laws without the Reichstag    ☐

---

**Hitler becomes Führer**

3 Write numbers in the boxes to order these events, from the earliest (1) to the latest (5).

  ☐    **A.** Hindenberg dies

  ☐    **B.** The Night of the Long Knives takes place

  ☐    **C.** Hitler announces army should swear allegiance to him as Führer

  ☐    **D.** Hitler invites Röhm and other SA leaders to a meeting at Bad Wiessee

  ☐    **E.** Röhm is murdered

---

**The Nazi police state**

4 Add **two** more examples of how the police state operated to each column of the table.

| SS (Nazi Party protection squad) | SD (Security service) | Gestapo (Secret police) |
| --- | --- | --- |
| •   Led by Himmler | •   Led by Heydrich | •   Set up by Goering, led by Heydrich |

5 Give **one** example of how the Nazi government controlled the legal system.

................................................................................................................................

6 Decide which statements are true and which are false. Circle your answers.

   **A.** Hitler didn't like the Catholic Church because Catholics were loyal to the Pope.    **True**    **False**

   **B.** There were two main Protestant Churches in Germany.    **True**    **False**

   **C.** The Confessing Church supported the Nazis.    **True**    **False**

   **D.** The Concordat was an agreement between Hitler and the Catholic Church.    **True**    **False**

   **E.** Hitler kept the terms of the Concordat.    **True**    **False**

# Nazi dictatorship, 1933–39

**Propaganda and censorship**

7 (a) When was the Reich Chamber of Culture set up? .................................................................

(b) State its main purpose.

........................................................................................................................................................

(c) Who oversaw its operations? .................................................................................................

**How popular was the Nazi regime?**

8 Fill in the gaps to complete this paragraph about support for the Nazis.

Once Hitler took power in ........................................, most Germans ........................................

Nazi leadership. One reason for this was that the Nazis reduced ........................................ and

Hitler's ........................................ policy was successful. Another reason was that censorship and

........................................ meant people only heard ........................................ messages

about the Nazis. It also meant that many people who were ........................................ to the Nazis

were afraid to speak out, although several groups opposed the Nazis in secret.

**Opposition to the Nazis**

9 Decide which statements are true and which are false. Circle your answers.

A. The Confessing Church opposed Nazi interference.     **True**     **False**
B. Martin Niemöller founded the Confessing Church.     **True**     **False**
C. Niemöller did not vote for the Nazis in 1933.     **True**     **False**
D. 400 Catholic priests were imprisoned for opposing the Nazis.     **True**     **False**

10 Which **three** of these were ways that young people like the Swing Youth and the Edelweiss Pirates rebelled against Nazi rule? Tick (✓) the correct answers.

A. Copying American fashions that the Nazis opposed ☐

B. Writing anti-Nazi graffiti ☐

C. Distributing anti-Nazi publications ☐

D. Attacking the Hitler Youth ☐

**Revision Guide**

How did you do? Go to pages 14–20 of the Revision Guide to remind yourself of any points you aren't sure about, and for more about this key topic.

# Nazi Germany, 1933–39

This key topic is about life in Nazi Germany in the years 1933–39. It includes Nazi policies towards women, the young and employment, changes in living standards and the persecution of minorities.

## Nazi policies towards women

1 Complete the table below. Add **two** more examples to each column.

| The Nazis believed that a woman should: | They believed that a woman should not: |
| --- | --- |
| • Stay at home with their family | • Go out to work |

2 Draw lines to match the belief on the left with the policy on the right. (Careful! Some beliefs match more than one policy.)

| | |
| --- | --- |
| **A.** Women should not work | **i.** Marriage loans |
| **B.** Women should get married | **ii.** Women were banned from public sector jobs |
| **C.** Women should have lots of children | **iii.** German Women's Enterprise |

## Nazi policies towards the young

3 Decide which statements are true and which are false. Circle your answers.

    **A.** All children had to join Nazi youth organisations from the age of 10.     **True**     **False**

    **B.** The League of German Maidens was for girls aged 10–14.     **True**     **False**

    **C.** Young people were expected to report people who opposed the Nazis.     **True**     **False**

    **D.** Activities reflected Nazi ideas about the roles of men and women.     **True**     **False**

    **E.** Activities like hiking and camping were for boys only.     **True**     **False**

## Nazi control of education

4 Which of these were ways that the Nazis controlled teachers? Tick (✓) the correct answers.

    **A.** They had to be Nazi Party members ☐

    **B.** They had to join the Nazi Teachers' League ☐

    **C.** From 1935 they had to use approved textbooks ☐

    **D.** They attended courses about Nazi ideas ☐

5 Give **two** examples of how school subjects promoted Nazi ideals.

    • ............................................................................................................

    • ............................................................................................................

6 Give **one** example of how propaganda was used in schools.

    ............................................................................................................

# Nazi Germany, 1933–39

**Policies to reduce unemployment**

7  List **two** policies that the Nazis put in place to reduce unemployment.

- .................................................................................................................................

- .................................................................................................................................

8  Draw lines to match the policy on the left with the aim on the right.

| A. Labour Front | i. Improve workplaces |
| B. Strength through Joy | ii. Oversee all German workers |
| C. Beauty of Labour | iii. Increase productivity by making workers happy |

**The treatment of minorities**

9  Fill in the gaps to complete this paragraph about Nazi racial beliefs and policies.

Hitler believed that Aryans were destined to be a ........................................ race'. Non-Aryans

(Roma and ........................................ people, Slavs, black people and Jews) were seen as

'........................................' or sub-humans. Hitler wanted to increase the number of 'pure'

Germans, so Aryans were expected to ........................................ other Aryans. Other groups

were called 'undesirable' – homosexuals were imprisoned, and mentally handicapped people were

........................................ .

**The persecution of the Jews**

10  Give **two** examples of how the Nuremberg Laws (1935) made it easier for the Nazis to persecute Jewish people in Germany.

- .................................................................................................................................

- .................................................................................................................................

11  In **one** sentence, state what happened on Kristallnacht, 9–10 November 1938.

.................................................................................................................................

.................................................................................................................................

**Revision Guide**

How did you do? Go to pages 21–28 of the Revision Guide to remind yourself of any points you aren't sure about, and for more about this key topic.

# In the exam

After all your revision and preparation, you want to do well. There are some key things you should remember in the exam.

## What should I take with me?

- You must write in **black**, so it is a good idea to have more than one black pen with you.
- You might want a highlighter to mark the key words in the questions.
- Don't fill your desk with loads of other things – you know you won't need a calculator, for example, so leave it in your bag.
- Don't bother with correction fluid – just cross out any mistakes.

## Where should I start?

Start with the front cover of your exam paper.

- The most important bit is the space for your name – don't forget to write it!
- It tells you how much time you have for the exam.
- For Paper 3, it will remind you about the separate Sources/Interpretations Booklet. Make sure you have been given this.
- It will tell you which questions you must answer, and which ones you can choose.

## How can I stay focused?

1. Take deep, slow breaths at the start of the exam and to help you to focus as you work through the paper.
2. Highlight the key words in the questions, like dates, to make sure you focus on the right thing.
3. Plan your answers, especially for the longer essay questions. Work out what you want to say before you start writing.
4. If you get stuck, try a new question and come back to the other one later. Or make a list of what you do know about the topic in the question to help you get started.

## How can I manage my time?

- It is a good idea to divide your time. Spend more time on questions that are worth more marks. You could even write on the paper (on the front cover or next to each question) the time you will start each question before you begin answering.
- Check the time regularly to make sure that you still have enough time for the longer answers.
- If you haven't finished answering a low-mark question but you are running out of time, move on to a higher-mark question. You can come back to it if you need to.

## How much should I write?

- Your exam paper will give you space to write in for each question.
- Use the number of marks as a guide to how much you should write – a 12-mark question will need more than a 4-mark one.
- You don't always need to fill the space – this does not necessarily mean more marks.

## How should I check my work?

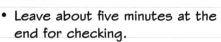

- Leave about five minutes at the end for checking.
- Check that you didn't miss any questions.
- Check your spelling and punctuation.
- Check that you have not made any obvious mistakes, like using the wrong date.

---

If you run out of space to finish an answer, **ask for more paper**. Don't use the answer space for the next question – this will make your answer hard to read. If you use extra paper, write 'answer on extra paper' at the bottom of the answer space. Then write the question number on the extra paper and complete your answer. At the end, check any extra paper has your name on it and that it is clear which answers you have finished there.

**Had a look** ☐   **Nearly there** ☐   **Nailed it!** ☐

# Writing clear answers

The most important thing in the exam is writing down the correct information, but it also helps to write clear, well-organised answers. This will make your answers easier to follow.

## Get the basics right

✓ Use a good, **black** pen.

✓ Use paragraphs – they will help to make your points clearer.

✓ Write in the correct answer spaces. If you use extra paper, add a label to the new page to make it clear which question you are continuing. Write 'answer on extra paper' where you ran out of space.

✓ If you make a mistake, cross it out neatly.

## How can I write clearly?

1 Always write in Standard English – formal language, not slang.

2 Use adverbials or linking phrases to connect ideas and make your meaning clear – such as, 'for example', 'however', 'therefore', 'as a result', 'consequently', 'in addition', 'significantly', 'in contrast', 'similarly'.

3 Use key terms for the topic.

## Does my handwriting matter?

Your work will be marked, no matter what your handwriting is like. **However**, it is always a good idea to write as neatly as you can to make sure all the words in your answer are clear.

Imagine you had to mark these sentences. Which is easiest to read?

*One reason for this is*

*One reason for this is*

## Should I plan my answers?

Plans help you to organise your ideas.

✗ **4-mark questions** – you won't spend much time on these, so you don't need a plan.

✓ **8-mark questions** – you might find it helpful to jot down a quick plan, such as a short list of points to include.

✓ **12-mark and 16-mark questions** – make a plan for these questions. Many of the best exam answers for these questions have plans.

There are different ways to plan. You can see examples on pages 25, 29 and 41.

**Top tip**

## How can I write effective paragraphs?

A good way to write effective paragraphs is to use **PEEL – Point, Evidence, Explain, Link.**

**POINT** – say what the paragraph is about.

**EVIDENCE** – give examples.

**EXPLAIN** – say what the evidence shows.

**LINK** – connect back to the question. This paragraph is answering the question 'Explain why support for the Nazis grew in the years 1929–32.'

One reason that support for the Nazis grew in the years 1929–32 was that Hitler presented himself as a strong leader. He gave speeches around the country and on the radio, and his image appeared on most publicity material. The Depression had left many suffering terrible poverty. As a result, they saw the Weimar government as weak and were looking for a strong leader. Many people were persuaded by Hitler that he could solve the economic crisis, and consequently they turned to the Nazis.

**Had a look** ☐   **Nearly there** ☐   **Nailed it!** ☐

# Working with sources

You need to know how to look at sources and how to work with them in the exam.

## What is a source?

A source is a piece of historical evidence from the time period you are looking at.

> When you read or examine a source look for three things:
> - What is the source about?
> - Is there an opinion or a message in the source?
> - Does the source agree with or challenge what you know about the topic?

**Top tip**

## What sources are in the exam?

- In the Paper 3 exam, there will be three sources. You will find Source A with Question 1 in the exam paper, and Sources B and C in a separate Sources/Interpretations Booklet.

- At least one of the sources will be a written source (like a diary entry or a speech). The other two could be written sources or images (like posters or photographs).

## Analysing the content of a source

**Source B:** From an article for a Nazi paper, written in May 1933 by Achim Gercke, who was a Nazi official.

> Scattering the Jews to the four winds does not solve the <u>Jewish Question</u>, but rather makes it worse. A systematic <u>program of settlement</u>, therefore, is the best solution.
>
> Plans and programs must have a goal pointing to the future. They may not be focused only on a temporarily unpleasant situation. A better future demands the systematic solution of the Jewish Question, not the organization of the Jews.
>
> We must build our state without the Jews. They can be only <u>stateless foreigners</u> among us, with no legal permanent standing.

About: the Nazis blamed the Jews for Germany's problems and wanted to get rid of them.

Agrees with what I know: the Nazis moved Jews to ghettos and settlements.

Message: even Jews born in Germany would be treated as foreigners.

**Source C:** An illustration from 1936 showing the different badges worn by inmates in the concentration camp at Dachau. The categories of prisoner are: political, criminals, foreign forced labourers, Jehovah's Witnesses, homosexuals and 'asocial' people.

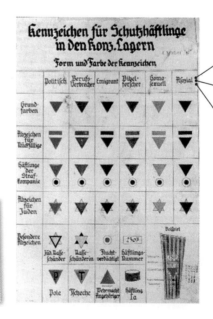

> Annotate or highlight key points in the sources as you read or look at them. This will help you to find ideas to include in your answer.

About: the categories of Nazi prisoners.

Message: none of these people were welcome in German society.

Agrees with my knowledge: the Nazis persecuted many different groups of people.

**Had a look** ☐   **Nearly there** ☐   **Nailed it!** ☐

# Working with sources

## How can I spot a message in a source?

**1** Look at the words that have been chosen. Are they positive (like victory or success) or negative (like disaster or failure)?

**2** Does the source exaggerate anything? Does it only give examples from one point of view?

**3** In illustrations, has the artist made anyone look smart and intelligent, or stupid and ridiculous?

Most sources were not made just to share information. They were designed to share an opinion, to persuade others that something was good or bad, or to make people support something. A historian needs to learn to spot the message.

In Paper 3, you will handle sources in these questions: 1 (which asks you to make inferences from a source); 3a (which is about the usefulness of the sources); 3c (where you may use sources in your explanation). You can find more about these questions on pages 19–22, 27–30 and 35–38.

## Provenance: nature, origin and purpose

The **provenance** of a source is its **nature**, **origin** and **purpose**.

| Nature | What type of source is it? | For example, is it a newspaper article, speech, leaflet, letter, diary entry, book, postcard, poster, cartoon or photograph? |
|---|---|---|
| Origin | Where is it from? | Who wrote it? Were they involved with the event? Is it from before, after or during the event? Is it from where the events happened or from somewhere else? |
| Purpose | Why was it made? | Was it made to inform people? Persuade people? Sell something? Give evidence to make a decision?<br>Was it made for the public or for a specific person or group of people? |

Identifying the nature, origin and purpose (NOP) of a source is an important skill. It will help you to evaluate the usefulness of a source. For Paper 3, you will need this skill for Question 3a.

## Where can I find the provenance?

Start by looking at the key information about provenance that comes just before the source itself. This can give you a lot of information:

• what the source is

• who made or wrote it

• when they made or wrote it.

Always read the key information about provenance first. The source itself may have information about NOP too, but starting with the key information will help you to spot words or details in the source which show the opinion or message of the person who created it.

**Top tip**

The source is part of an article.

**Source B:** Part of an article for a Nazi paper, written in May 1933 by Achim Gercke, who was a Nazi official.

It was written for a Nazi paper.

It was written by a former Nazi official.

It was written in May 1933, after the Nazis had come to power.

**Had a look** ☐ **Nearly there** ☐ **Nailed it!** ☐

# Working with interpretations

Using interpretations is an important skill for your Paper 3 exam. You need to know how to look at interpretations and how to work with them in the exam.

## What is an interpretation?

An interpretation is a modern historian's opinion or judgement about a person, event or development in history. The historian will usually have researched the event or period using sources from that time.

You can find out more about working with sources on pages 11 and 12.

## What interpretations are in the Paper 3 exam?

- There will be two interpretations. You will find them in a separate Sources/Interpretations Booklet.
- The interpretations in Paper 3 will both be written interpretations. They are most likely to be short extracts from a history book.

## What is the difference between an interpretation and a source?

**Interpretations are not the same as sources.** A source is a piece of historical evidence from the time period you are looking at. An interpretation is produced **after** that time period, by a historian writing about the topic years later, using sources from the period as evidence.

In the exam, make sure you remember that interpretations and sources are different. For interpretations:
- You **don't** need to say whether they are reliable or not.
- You **don't** need to discuss who wrote them, when they wrote them or what the book or publication was called.

**Top tip**

## Interpretations and viewpoints

Just like the rest of us, historians don't always agree with each other. When they study the past, each historian forms their own opinions and makes their own judgements about it. One historian might think that something was good, but a different historian might think the same thing was bad. One historian might think that something was more important than something else, but a different historian might think the exact opposite. So different historians form different interpretations of the past.

## How can I tell what the historian's viewpoint is?

Read the interpretation **carefully**. Then ask yourself:

1 Do they say that something was more or less important?

2 Do they focus on a particular part of the topic?

3 Have they ignored another part of the topic?

4 Do they use strong words that indicate an opinion, like success, failure, victory, disaster or others?

In Paper 3, you will be asked about interpretations in these questions:
- 3b, which asks you to identify the main difference between the viewpoints
- 3c, which asks you to say why the viewpoints are different
- 3d, which asks you to evaluate one interpretation, using both interpretations and your own knowledge.

You can find more about these questions on pages 31–42.

**Had a look** ☐    **Nearly there** ☐    **Nailed it!** ☐

# Working with interpretations

## Analysing the content of an interpretation

Annotate or highlight key points in the interpretations as you read them. This will help you to find ideas to include in your answer.

The Nazis targeted a range of racial groups they thought were inferior.

The Nazis wanted to remove anyone who threatened their ideas of racial purity.

The Nazis removed opposition to their ideology by targeting people with different political and religious beliefs.

**Interpretation 1:** From the website of the Holocaust Memorial Day Trust, an organisation which supports Holocaust Memorial Day to remember those, including six million Jews, murdered by the Nazis. This text is from 2019.

The Nazis believed Aryan people were superior to all others. [This] partly explains their hatred towards Jews, Roma and Sinti people (sometimes referred to as 'Gypsies') and black people. Slavic people, such as those from Poland and Russia, were considered inferior and were targeted because they lived in areas needed for German expansion.

The Nazis wanted to 'improve' the genetic make-up of the population and so persecuted people they deemed to be disabled, either mentally or physically, as well as gay people. Political opponents, primarily communists, trade unionists and social democrats, as well as those whose religious beliefs conflicted with Nazi ideology, such as Jehovah's Witnesses, were also targeted for persecution.

In 1938, the Nazi persecution of the Jews got worse as they started to resettle them by force.

The persecution even targeted the most vulnerable.

Kristallnacht, 9–10 November 1938 – a deliberate and violent attack on Jewish communities.

The Jews were punished for the trouble on Kristallnacht even though they were the victims.

**Interpretation 2:** From the website of Yad Vashem, the World Holocaust Remembrance Center. Yad Vashem is a leading centre of education and research. This text describes the events of 1938 and is from 2019.

The crackdown on Jews took on an increased ferocity… On October 27, 1938, Nazi Germany carried out the brutal eviction of Jews with Polish citizenship – the first mass deportation of Jews. SS men drove children, elderly, and the sick across the Polish border. [This deportation] was directly connected with the pogrom[1] of Kristallnacht. During the pogrom 91 Jews were murdered, more than 1400 synagogues across Germany and Austria were torched, and Jewish-owned shops and businesses were plundered and destroyed. In addition, the Jews were forced to pay "compensation" for the damage that had been caused and approximately 30 000 Jews were arrested and sent to concentration camps.

[1]**pogrom:** a violent attack on an ethnic or religious group.

When you read the interpretations, try to pick out the tone that the author has used – that is, the way that they have used words to show their opinion. For example, Interpretation 2 uses words like 'brutal eviction'.

Top tip

**Had a look** ☐   **Nearly there** ☐   **Nailed it!** ☐

# Using key terms

Using key terms helps to show you know and understand the topic.

## What key terms might I need to use?

**abdication** – when a leader like a king, queen or emperor gives up their role

**armistice** – an agreement to stop fighting, made by countries who are at war with each other

**Aryan** – the people of northern Europe who the Nazis believed were superior and a 'master race'

**autobahn** – the German word for motorway

**censorship** – the banning of information or ideas

**Chancellor** – the German equivalent of a Prime Minister

**communism** – a political and economic system in which representatives of the workers set up a government and take over ownership of all land, property and resources in a country

**concentration camp** – a prison where large numbers of people are forced to provide labour

**depression** – when the economy collapses and a country has very little money

**Gestapo** – the secret police in Nazi Germany

**hyperinflation** – when prices rise hugely and very quickly as money loses its value

**Freikorps** – a right-wing group of former soldiers who tried to overthrow the government in 1920

**Führer** – a German word for 'leader'

**Kaiser** – the German word for 'Emperor'

**Lebensraum** – a German word meaning 'living space', which was used by the Nazis to justify plans to invade countries on the eastern border of Germany to get more land

**Mein Kampf** – a book written by Adolf Hitler in the 1920s setting out his political beliefs. The title is German for 'My Struggle'

**nationalism** – a political system in which all policies are organised to make the nation stronger and more independent

**propaganda** – information, usually biased, designed to influence public opinion

**putsch** – a violent attempt to overthrow a government

**Reichstag** – the name of the German parliament

**Rentenmark** – a currency issued in 1923 to control hyperinflation

**reparations** – compensation paid after a war by a defeated nation to the winning nation(s)

**SA (Sturmabteilung)** – a force who provided protection for Nazi rallies and disrupted the opposition

**socialism** – a political system which says that a country's land, industries and wealth should all belong to the workers of that country

**Spartacists** – a left-wing group of activists who organised an unsuccessful revolt in 1919

**SS (Schutzstaffel)** – the main Nazi agency of security, surveillance and terror

**Untermenschen** – in Hitler's hierarchy of races, people who were classified as 'sub-human'

Take extra care with German words like **Reichstag** and with names like **Stresemann, von Schleicher, Röhm, Goering** and **Goebbels**.

The key terms with capital letters will always use capital letters wherever they appear in a sentence.

The key terms on this page are the most important ones. If you think of others, write them down in the back of this book.

**Had a look** ☐   **Nearly there** ☐   **Nailed it!** ☐

# SPaG

Good spelling, punctuation and grammar (SPaG) are important in every exam, but in your Paper 3 exam, four marks are available specifically for SPaG and your use of specialist terminology.

## What are the SPaG marks for?

For Paper 3, SPaG is tested on Question 3d.

You can get up to four marks for your quality of written communication.

The best responses:

- ✓ have accurate spelling and punctuation throughout the answer
- ✓ use the rules of grammar to write clearly throughout the answer
- ✓ use a wide range of key terms.

## What about key terms?

Use key terms to show your topic knowledge, like 'hyperinflation' in the stronger example below.

> ✗ In 1923, a major problem was that money became worth a lot less.

> ✓ In 1923, hyperinflation became a major problem.

## Tricky words

Some important words are often spelled incorrectly. Make sure you can spell these words:

| | | |
|---|---|---|
| armistice | beginning | benefited |
| exaggerate | government | Führer |
| occurred | persecution | purpose |
| preparation | putsch | Reichstag |

When you find other tricky words, list them at the back of this book.

## Formal language

| Use... | ✓ | ✗ |
|---|---|---|
| Standard English, not slang | currency | dosh |
| Correct grammar | would have | would of |

Use homophones (words that sound the same but have different meanings) correctly. For example, make sure you know whether to use 'their' or 'there'.

**Top tip**

## Writing clear sentences

Sentences that are clear start with capital letters, end with full-stops and are not too long.

> ✗ On 27 February 1933, the Reichstag building was set on fire and Hitler used this as an excuse to blame the Communist Party and as a result 4000 communists were arrested.

> ✓ On 27 February 1933, the Reichstag building was set on fire. Hitler used this as an excuse to blame the Communist Party. As a result, 4000 communists were arrested.

This example, with shorter sentences, is easier to read.

## Punctuation for meaning

Use punctuation to make your meaning clear:

- Use commas to separate ideas or information.
- Use commas between items in a list.
- Use apostrophes to show that something belongs to something else.

The comma shows that the Nazis were using boycotts and violence, not the Jews.

> ✓ The Nazis persecuted the Jews, using boycotts and violence. Hitler's beliefs meant he was keen to increase the number of 'pure' Germans.

The apostrophe shows that the beliefs belonged to Hitler.

**Had a look** ☐ **Nearly there** ☐ **Nailed it!** ☐

# Understanding your exam

It is a good idea to understand how your exam paper works. You will know what to expect and this will help you to feel confident when you are in the exam.

## Paper 3 modern depth study

Your modern depth study is your Paper 3 exam. Paper 3 is...

 a written exam

 1 hour 20 minutes

 worth 52 marks

 worth 30% of your GCSE History.

## What will I get in the exam?

- You will get an exam paper. The paper has spaces for you to write your answers in.
- For Paper 3, you will be given two booklets – one is your exam paper and one contains the sources and interpretations you will need to refer to.
- You will be given both booklets at the same time.

## What is a modern depth study?

This paper – Weimar and Nazi Germany, 1918–39 – explores a part of modern history. It is called a depth study because the time period it covers is quite a short one (1918–39), and it covers that time period in a lot of detail.

## What historical skills does my Paper 3 modern depth study assess?

Your GCSE History exam papers are designed to assess different historical skills, or 'assessment objectives' (AOs).

Your Paper 3 modern depth study will assess all four assessment objectives:

**AO1** – Demonstrate knowledge and understanding of the key features of the period.

This means you need to show your knowledge of the topic, including details of the main events, people and themes.

**AO2** – Explain and analyse events using second-order historical concepts.

This means you need to analyse historical ideas in your answers – these ideas are called **second-order historical concepts**.

The second-order historical concepts are: causation (why things happened), consequences (the results of something), similarity, difference, change, continuity (staying the same) and significance (how important an event, idea or change was).

**AO3** – Analyse, evaluate and use sources to make substantiated judgements.

This means you need to use historical sources to investigate a topic, and make judgements about how useful they are.

**Substantiated** means something that is backed up. A substantiated judgement is a judgement which is supported with a reason.

You can find out more about working with sources on pages 11–12.

**AO4** – Analyse, evaluate and make substantiated judgements about interpretations.

This means you need to understand and compare the interpretations, or opinions, of modern historians, and make a judgement whether or not you agree with their viewpoints.

You can find out more about working with interpretations on pages 13–14.

**Had a look** ☐  **Nearly there** ☐  **Nailed it!** ☐

# Understanding your exam

## What type of questions will be on the exam paper for Paper 3?

The questions for your modern depth study will always follow the same pattern:

---

**SECTION A**

1   Give **two** things you can infer from Source A about…

    **(4 marks)**

---

**Question 1** is the **making inferences** question:

- (4) Worth 4 marks
- Q Tests AO3
- ⏱ Spend about 5 minutes
- ✓ Give details about **two** things you can infer.

---

2   Explain why…

    **(12 marks)**

---

**Question 2** is the **explaining why** question:

- (12) Worth 12 marks
- Q Tests AO1 and AO2
- ⏱ Spend about 18 minutes
- ✓ You must use some of your own information.

---

**SECTION B**

**3a  Study Sources B and C.**

How useful are Sources B and C for an enquiry into…?

    **(8 marks)**

---

**Question 3a** is the **assessing usefulness** question:

- (8) Worth 8 marks
- Q Tests AO3
- ⏱ Spend about 12 minutes
- ✓ Use both sources and your own knowledge.

---

**3b  Study Interpretations 1 and 2…**

What is the main difference between these views?

    **(4 marks)**

---

**Question 3b** is the **identifying and explaining differences** question:

- (4) Worth 4 marks
- Q Tests AO4
- ⏱ Spend about 5 minutes
- ✓ Use details from both interpretations.

---

**3c  Suggest one reason why Interpretations 1 and 2 give different views about…**

    **(4 marks)**

---

**Question 3c** is the **suggesting reasons** question:

- (4) Worth 4 marks
- Q Tests AO4
- ⏱ Spend about 5 minutes
- ✓ Suggest one reason for the different views.

---

**3d  How far do you agree with Interpretation 2 about…**

    **(16 marks plus 4 marks for SPaG and use of specialist terminology)**

---

**Question 3d** is the **evaluating interpretations** question:

- (16) + (4) Worth 16 marks, plus 4 for SPaG
- Q Tests AO4
- ⏱ Spend about 30 minutes
- ✓ Use both interpretations and your knowledge.

---

**Had a look** ☐   **Nearly there** ☐   **Nailed it!** ☐

# Understanding Question 1

Question 1 will always be structured in the same way. Make sure you know how this question works and what it is asking you to do.

## How does Question 1 work?

This tells you that you need to infer **two** separate things from the source.

This question will always ask you to 'infer'.

In the exam, Source A will appear just before Question 1. For this example question, you will find Source A below.

This is the topic for the question. Look out for the word 'about' to help you identify the topic you need to focus on.

> **1** Give **two** things you can infer from Source A about the Nazis' vision for Germany's future.
>
> Complete the table below to explain your answer.
>
> **(4 marks)**

This question gives you a table to complete – you should use this to structure your answer.

Check how many marks the question is worth. This will help you to manage your time.

---

**Source A:** A Nazi poster published in 1935. The caption reads 'Hitler is building. Help out. Buy German goods.'

## What does Question 1 assess?

- ✓ Question 1 tests Assessment Objective 3.
- ✓ You need to show your ability to analyse sources.
- ✓ You will need to give examples of what you can infer from the source, and details from the source that support your inferences.

Take a look at page 17 for more about the assessment objectives.

## How long should I spend?

Spend about 5 minutes on Question 1.

Try not to spend longer as the next questions will need plenty of time.

---

## What does 'infer' mean?

To **infer** means to work out something that isn't directly written or shown. You need to read between the lines – or look beneath the surface details, if the source is an image – and think about what the source suggests about the topic.

**Top tip**

You **must** make sure that both your inferences are connected to the topic in the question.

**Top tip**

Make sure both your inferences are **based on the content of the source**, and not from the information about the provenance (origin) of the source that comes just before the source itself.

**Had a look** ☐  **Nearly there** ☐  **Nailed it!** ☐

# Understanding Question 1

## Inferences and supporting details

Your answer should give two valid inferences, and give supporting evidence from the source for each one. For example, for the question on page 19 about the Nazis' vision for Germany's future you could give this inference and supporting detail:

> **What I can infer:**
> It will be a strong country.

This is a **valid inference** from the source. It is connected to the topic question and is based on the content of the source. This would get one mark.

> **Details in the source that tell me this:**
> The man in the poster is tall and muscular and the wall is made up of large, heavy bricks.

This is **supporting detail** from the source. The supporting detail can quote or paraphrase words in the source, or be a valid comment about it. This would get one mark.

## How is Question 1 marked?

Marks are available for making the inferences and for providing supporting detail:

✓ There is **one mark available for each valid inference** you make – so one mark for making one inference, and two marks for making two inferences. Adding more inferences does not improve your mark.

✓ There is **one mark available** for adding supporting detail from the source to one of your inferences, and **two marks** if you add supporting detail to both inferences.

## Using the table format

The answer space for this question is in a table format and you should write your answer into this table.

- The words 'What I can infer' in the table tell you where to write each inference.
- The words 'Details in the source that tell me this' in the table tell you where to add the supporting detail for each inference.
- Use the space in the table as a guide to how much to write – you should keep your answers short.

## Top tips for success

**Top tip**

✓ Make **two different inferences** – take care not to make the same one twice.

✓ Make **valid** inferences – make sure that both inferences are **connected to the topic** in the question.

✓ Base your inferences on the **content of the source**, not the information about the provenance.

✓ For each inference, **add supporting detail** from the source.

✓ Keep your answers **concise** – don't write more than you need to.

✓ **Use the table** on the exam paper – there will be spaces marked for each inference and for each supporting detail.

**Had a look** ☐    **Nearly there** ☐    **Nailed it!** ☐

# Answering Question 1

You need to understand how you can write a successful answer to Question 1.

## Reading the question

1 Give **two** things you can infer from Source A about the Nazis' vision for Germany's future.

Complete the table below to explain your answer.

**(4 marks)**

Always read the question carefully before you start writing your answer. Make sure you are clear about what the enquiry in the question is.

Short, 4-mark questions do not need a plan.

## Steps to success

**1** Make **one valid inference** from the source.

(i) What I can infer

The Nazis will be a central part of Germany's future.

Write each part of your answer in the correct space in the table.

Make one valid inference which is connected to the enquiry.

**2** Add detail from the source to support your first inference.

Details in the source that tell me this:

The Nazi flag with the swastika is pictured in the background.

Add supporting detail from the source for your first inference.

The supporting detail could be a quotation, paraphrase or valid comment on a feature of the source. This example comments on a feature.

**3** Make a **second valid inference** from the source.

(ii) What I can infer:

They want to rebuild Germany to make it strong.

Make a second inference which is connected to the enquiry.

Focus on the content of the source, rather than on its provenance.

**4** Add detail from the source to support your second inference.

Details in the source that tell me this:

The man in the poster is building a strong wall using large, sturdy bricks.

Add supporting detail.

Make sure the detail you choose supports your second inference.

**Had a look** ☐    **Nearly there** ☐    **Nailed it!** ☐

# Answering Question 1

## Getting it right

Question 1 should be a good chance to get some straightforward marks at the beginning of your exam paper. Stay focused on the question and don't write more than you need to.

---

(i) What I can infer:

The Nazi flag is an important symbol.

Details in the source that tell me this:

The Nazi flag is positioned in the background between the field and the image of the man building the wall.

(ii) What I can infer:

They think farming is important to support Germany's rebuilding. **(1)**

Details in the source that tell me this:

The man building the strong wall is in the foreground of the poster.

✗ The first inference is not valid as it is not based on the enquiry in the question.

✗ The supporting detail is correct but, as it does not support a valid inference, it would get no marks.

✓ This is a valid inference.

✗ The supporting detail given is not linked to the inference.

---

(i) What I can infer:

Rebuilding is the most important task to make Germany strong. **(1)**

Details in the source that tell me this:

The muscular man who is rebuilding the wall is shown in the foreground of the poster. <u>This supports the inference because</u> it makes the man and the rebuilding the main focus of the poster, showing it is the most important thing. **(1)**

(ii) What I can infer:

<u>People are being told to buy German goods.</u>

Details in the source that tell me this:

The poster text tells people to 'Buy German goods'.

✓ This is a valid inference.

✗ This answer is correct and would get a mark, but it goes into too much detail about why the evidence supports the inference. You just need to focus on relevant supporting detail.

✗ This is not an inference – it paraphrases a detail of the source.

✗ The supporting detail is correct. However, as it does not support a valid inference, it would get no marks.

---

(i) What I can infer:

Germany will be able to provide most of its own food. **(1)**

Details in the source that tell me this:

The wagon in the field is piled high with crops. **(1)**

(ii) What I can infer:

They want all Germans to be involved in rebuilding the country. **(1)**

Details in the source that tell me this:

The poster text asks people to 'Help out'. **(1)**

✓ The first inference is a valid point about the source. It also has relevant supporting evidence from the source. So this would get 2 marks.

✓ This inference is valid and supported by correct evidence. This would also get 2 marks.

---

**Had a look** ☐     **Nearly there** ☐     **Nailed it!** ☐

# Understanding Question 2

Question 2 will always be structured in the same way. Make sure you know how this question works and what it is asking you to do.

## How does Question 2 work?

Identify the command phrase – this question will always ask you to 'explain why'.

This is the consequence that you need to explain.

If the question has dates, make sure that you write about the correct time period.

You **must** include at least one reason from your own knowledge.

> 2   Explain why support for the Nazis increased between 1929 and 1932.
>
>                                                        **(12 marks)**
>
> You may use the following in your answer:
>
> • unemployment
>
> • the SA
>
> You **must** also use information of your own.

Check how many marks the question is worth – this will help you to manage your time.

Look at the two suggestions – they might be helpful in deciding what to write about.

 **Links** This question is similar to Question 4 on Paper 1 (your thematic study) and Question 1b on Paper 2 (your British depth study).

## What does Question 2 assess?

✓ Question 2 tests Assessment Objectives 1 and 2.

✓ You need to show your knowledge of the topic.

✓ You also need to show you can explain and analyse **causation** (why events or changes happened).

Take a look at page 17 for more about the assessment objectives.

## How long should I spend?

Spend about 18 minutes on Question 2.

This question is worth 12 marks so leave yourself enough time to do a good job. But don't spend too long – you will need enough time for Questions 3a (8 marks) and 3d (16 marks) in particular.

## What does 'explain why' mean?

**Explaining why** means giving reasons for something. It is different to just describing a topic. For example, if you were asked 'what was school like today?' you would describe your day. But if you were asked 'why did you go to school today?' you would give reasons why you went to school. It is the same with this question – you need to write an analysis, giving three reasons that explain why the consequence in the question happened.

## What will Question 2 focus on?

Question 2 could ask you about any aspect of Weimar and Nazi Germany you have studied. It could be about a broad topic, like the example above (the increased support for the Nazis between 1929 and 1932), or a specific event, like Kristallnacht (9–10 November 1938). The question could ask you to explain: an event; a development; a success; a failure.

> The key thing to remember is that you need **three reasons** and each one needs to be **connected to the question topic**.

**Top tip**

**Had a look** ☐   **Nearly there** ☐   **Nailed it!** ☐

# Understanding Question 2

## Choosing reasons

Question 2 will always include two bullet points. **These bullet points are only suggestions – you don't have to use them.** This type of question will always have several possible reasons. If you don't know what one of the bullet points means, or you don't feel confident writing a paragraph about it, you can replace it with a reason of your own.

For example, the question on page 23 suggests 'unemployment' and 'the SA'. If you were answering this question, you could write about these reasons. However, you need **three** reasons in your answer, so you would need to add at least one idea of your own – for example, the impact of propaganda, Hitler's personal appeal or anger at the Weimar government.

**Remember:** Even if you replace one or both bullet points with another reason, you still need to give **three reasons** overall. At least one of the reasons needs to be your own information.

## How is Question 2 marked?

Strong answers to Question 2:

- ✓ Give an analytical explanation which is tightly focused on the question throughout.
- ✓ Keep the explanation clear and well organised throughout.
- ✓ Include information that is accurate, relevant and closely linked to the question.
- ✓ Show a wide range of knowledge and understanding of the topic.

## Using language to write clear answers

To make your answer clear, you could start each paragraph like this:

One reason was…

A second reason was…

A third reason was…

## Writing analytically

You need to make sure you are **explaining why**. This is called writing analytically. Use phrases like these to show how each reason led to the consequence in the question:

- This led to…
- As a result…
- Consequently…
- This increased/reduced…
- This showed that…

Remember to use **key terms** in your answer.

Turn to page 10 for more about writing clear answers. You can find examples of key terms on page 15.

You don't need to write an introduction or a conclusion for Question 2.

## Top tips for success

**Top tip**

- ✓ Give **three reasons** in your explanation.
- ✓ Include **information of your own**.
- ✓ **Plan** your answer before you write – this will help you to stay focused on the question throughout your answer.
- ✓ Structure your answer clearly using **PEEL paragraphs**.
- ✓ **Explain clearly** why each reason you include caused the consequence in the question.
- ✓ Support each reason with **clear and accurate information** about the topic.
- ✓ If the question includes a date range (for example, 'between 1929 and 1932'), only include information from that period.

**Top tip**

**Had a look** ☐ **Nearly there** ☐ **Nailed it!** ☐

24

# Answering Question 2

You need to understand how you can write a successful answer to Question 2.

## Reading the question

> 2 Explain why <u>support for the Nazis increased</u> between 1929 and 1932.
>
> **(12 marks)**
>
> You may use the following in your answer:
>
> • unemployment
>
> • the SA
>
> You **must** also use information of your own.

Always read the question carefully before you start writing your answer. Make sure you are clear on the topic.

Check the number of marks. This will help you to use your time well in the exam.

## How can I structure my answer?

**1** Write about your first reason in one PEEL paragraph.

**2** Write about your second reason in one PEEL paragraph.

**3** Write about your third reason in one PEEL paragraph.

Remember **PEEL: Point – Evidence – Explain – Link**

You can find out more about paragraphing and the PEEL structure on page 10.

## Plan your answer

This question is worth 12 marks, so take a minute or two to make a quick plan before you start writing.

> 1. Unemployment
>    • 6 million unemployed + workers wages cut = poverty
>    • Government measures ineffective
>
> 2. The SA
>    • Made Nazis look disciplined and reliable
>    • Disrupted opposition meetings
>
> 3. Propaganda
>    • Targeted many sectors of society
>    • Pushed idea of united nation

The best answers are well-organised, with three paragraphs. Structure your plan to reflect this.

Number the points in your plan so you have an order for your answer.

Keep your plan short and simple. You don't need to write in full sentences.

Remember to include your own knowledge in the plan. This plan includes a third reason which was not mentioned in the question.

This is one style of plan. You can see other plans on pages 29, 41, 60, 63 and 68.

**Had a look** [ ] **Nearly there** [ ] **Nailed it!** [ ]

# Answering Question 2

## Steps to success

**1** Write a paragraph about your first point. Remember to use PEEL to structure your paragraph clearly.

One reason that more people supported the Nazis was rising unemployment. The Wall Street Crash in 1929 meant that the USA stopped lending money to Germany, and wanted its loans repaid. This meant that businesses couldn't afford to employ as many people. Unemployment increased from 1.3m in 1929 to 6.1m in 1933. The people who still had jobs were paid less. Many people were in terrible poverty and government policies did little to help, so people looked for alternatives. The Nazis promised to tackle unemployment, and consequently support for them increased.

Make a clear **point** at the start to show what the paragraph is about. This example uses one of the reasons given in the question.

Include some **evidence**. This example only uses a couple of points but it is enough to show understanding of the topic.

**Explain** how the reason caused the consequence (more support for the Nazis). This example uses 'so' to explain analytically.

**Link** back to the question.

**2** Write a paragraph about your second point. Keep focused on the question and use PEEL to structure your writing.

**Point**          **Evidence**

A second reason was the SA. There were 400 000 members of the SA by 1930. It was a large, uniformed force which was very organised and disciplined. This meant that many people felt they could trust the Nazis to sort out social unrest and make Germany stronger. The SA also disrupted opposition meetings, which made the opposition weaker. As a result, the SA helped to increase support for the Nazis.

**Explain** – here, the phrase 'This meant that' is used to write analytically.

**Link** back to the question.

**3** Write a paragraph about your third point. Remember to refer back to your plan and stay focused on explaining why.

A third reason was the Nazis' skilful use of propaganda. The Nazis used propaganda to target...

This meant that...

As a result, more people felt that Hitler was the answer to their problems and would make Germany strong, which led to an increase in support for the Nazis.

Always include **three** reasons. This paragraph is about a reason that was not suggested in the question – so it also uses the student's own knowledge.

**Had a look** ☐   **Nearly there** ☐   **Nailed it!** ☐

# Understanding Question 3a

Question 3a will always be structured in the same way. Make sure you know how this question works and what it is asking you to do.

## How does Question 3a work?

In the exam, Sources B and C will be in the separate Sources and Interpretations Booklet. For this example question, you will find Sources B and C on page 11.

Identify the command phrase – this question will always ask you to consider 'how useful' the sources are for a particular enquiry.

**3a** Study <u>Sources B and C</u> on page 11.

<u>How useful</u> are Sources B and C for an enquiry into <u>the persecution of minorities in Germany after 1933?</u>

Explain your answer, <u>using Sources B and C and your knowledge of the historical context.</u>

<u>(8 marks)</u>

This is the **enquiry** (area of investigation) you need to focus on. Make sure you pay attention to any dates in the question.

Check how many marks the question is worth – this will help you to manage your time.

 **Links** This question is similar to Question 2a on Paper 1 (your thematic study).

You must refer to both sources and use your own knowledge.

## What does Question 3a assess?

- ✓ Question 3a tests Assessment Objective 3.
- ✓ You need to use historical sources to investigate a topic.
- ✓ You need to make judgements about how useful the sources for the enquiry given in the question are.

## How long should I spend?

Spend about 12 minutes on Question 3a.

Remember that you need to look at **both** sources. Divide your time equally between them so you give them equal attention in your answer.

Take a look at page 17 for more about the assessment objectives.

## Why do I need to focus on the enquiry in the question?

Imagine a toolbox. It has different tools, such as hammers, screwdrivers and saws. Each tool is useful in one way or another. But **how** useful each tool is depends on the job you need to do. For example, if you need to hit a nail into a wall, a hammer is useful, whereas a saw is not – but if you need to cut a piece of wood, the saw is a very useful tool.

All sources are useful in some ways, but how useful they are will depend on the enquiry topic. For example, look at Source C on page 11. It is very useful for investigating some enquiries, like the sorts of people the Nazis imprisoned, but less useful for studying how people in Germany felt about the persecution of the Jews. So, **when you consider how useful the sources are for Question 3a, make sure you stay focused on the enquiry in the question.**

**Top tip**

**Had a look** ☐ **Nearly there** ☐ **Nailed it!** ☐

# Understanding Question 3a

## How to judge 'usefulness'

To judge **usefulness** you need to assess how useful the source is for the enquiry in the question.

To measure usefulness, you need to think about two things:

- How much can you learn about the enquiry topic from the content of the source?

- Is the source giving you accurate information?

## What's in the source?

Pick out points from the content of the source which give information about the enquiry topic. If the source contains information that is relevant then it is useful for the enquiry.

Compare the content to your own knowledge. If the source supports what you know about the topic, it is more useful.

**Remember:** Focus on what **is** in the source, not on what is missing. Missing content is only important if it should be in the source but isn't.

## Is the information accurate?

You need to consider whether the information in the source is accurate:

- Is it balanced? For example, a balanced, confidential account written for a government department making policies might be likely to contain accurate details.

- Or is it presenting the information in a one-sided or exaggerated way? For example, a newspaper cartoon which is criticising a politician might be exaggerated.

Generally, a source which is more accurate and more balanced will be more useful. However, if the enquiry is about people's opinions, sometimes a one-sided, exaggerated source is more useful for showing what people thought.

Look at the **provenance – nature, origin and purpose** – of the source. Does this make the source more or less useful?

You can find more about nature, origin and purpose on page 12.

**Remember:** A source can be useful even if it is unreliable (if you can't trust or believe it). For example, a cartoon criticising a politician is likely to be exaggerating the actions of that politician and is therefore a less reliable source. However, it would still be useful in an enquiry about people's opinions as it shows what some people thought about that politician's actions.

## How is Question 3a marked?

Strong answers to Question 3a:

- ☑ judge the usefulness of each source for the enquiry given in the question
- ☑ explain clearly how the provenance of each source makes it more or less useful
- ☑ support their judgements with comments on each source's content and provenance
- ☑ use own knowledge to interpret the sources and support their judgements.

You don't need to compare the sources and you don't need to decide which one is more useful. Write about one source, then the other – without comparing them.

## Top tips for success

- ✓ Stay focused on the enquiry given in the question – **decide how useful each source is for this enquiry.**

- ✓ Refer to **both sources** in your answer – make a judgement about the usefulness of each one.

- ✓ Analyse the **content** and **provenance** of each source – **explain why** this makes the source more or less useful.

- ✓ Use **your own knowledge of the topic** to judge the source – does it agree with what you know?

- ✓ Make a **quick plan** before you write to help you to stay focused.

**Had a look** ☐   **Nearly there** ☐   **Nailed it!** ☐

# Answering Question 3a

You need to understand how you can write a successful answer to Question 3a.

## Reading the question

3a Study Sources B and C on page 11.

How useful are Sources B and C for an enquiry into the persecution of minorities in Germany after 1933?

Explain your answer, using Sources B and C and your knowledge of the historical context.

(8 marks)

Always read the question carefully before you start writing your answer.

Make sure you are clear about what the enquiry topic of the question is, including any dates.

**Top tip**

### Writing about usefulness

Use phrases such as 'quite useful', 'very useful' and 'partially useful' to give a clear judgement about the usefulness of a source.

**Remember:** No source in the exam will ever be useless for the enquiry. You can say it is not very useful but don't say it is useless.

## How can I structure my answer?

① Explain how useful the content of **Source B** is for the enquiry topic. Use at least one example from the source.

② Explain how the provenance affects the usefulness of **Source B**. Finish with an overall judgement about usefulness.

③ Repeat Steps 1 and 2 for **Source C**.

**Top tip**

Remember that you don't need to compare the sources.

You can find more about nature, origin and purpose on page 12.

## Plan your answer

This question is worth 8 marks, so note down a quick plan before you start writing.

| Source B | Source C |
|---|---|
| • Discusses 'Jewish Question' | • Multiple groups: political, criminal, religious and homosexual people |
| • Nazis began with forcing Jews into resettlements | • Produced by Nazis for use in concentration camps |
| • Written by Nazi official to be read by public | • Quite useful: shows different groups persecuted but no numbers |
| • Useful: shows Nazi attitude to Jews | |

The best answers are well-organised. Include clear notes about both sources in your plan.

Keep your plan short and simple. You don't need to write in full sentences.

Include quick points linked to your own knowledge – this will help you remember to include them in your answer.

You only need one point on NOP – purpose is often the most helpful.

Note down a quick judgement about each source – this will help you remember to include it in your answer.

**Had a look** ☐ **Nearly there** ☐ **Nailed it!** ☐

# Answering Question 3a

## Steps to success

**1** Explain how useful the content of **Source B** is for the enquiry topic in the question.

Source B is useful for an enquiry into the persecution of minorities in Germany after 1933. It argues that the best way to 'solve' the 'Jewish Question' is by forcing Jews into resettlement. This programme only began in 1939 with the introduction of ghettos after the invasion of Poland, so this source shows that 'solutions' like this were discussed much earlier. The source also says that Jews should be treated as 'stateless foreigners' with 'no legal permanent standing'. This is very similar to what was enacted in the Nuremberg Laws of September 1935. Again, it shows that Nazi persecution of Jews after 1933 was planned well in advance.

Start with a quick judgement about the usefulness of the source.

Pick out points from the content of the source which give information about the enquiry topic. You could include short, relevant quotations.

Use your own knowledge about the topic to explain how the content of the source fits with the enquiry topic.

Use key terms to show your knowledge of the topic.

Explain how your points are linked to the enquiry topic.

**2** Go on to explain how the provenance affects the usefulness of **Source B** for the enquiry topic in the question.

Source B is probably reliable evidence of what the Nazis thought about the Jews because it is part of an article written for a Nazi newspaper, by a former Nazi official. This means that the ideas in it are very unlikely to go against what the Nazi leadership thought. The source mentions two policies – depriving Jewish people of citizenship and a programme of settlement – that the Nazis eventually introduced. Therefore, this is a useful source but needs to be treated carefully. It was written for the public so could not state the true nature of the Nazis' plans.

Use NOP to help you decide whether the source is reliable or not – this answer uses the nature of the source.

Explain how this affects the usefulness of the source.

Finish your analysis of Source B with an overall judgement about its usefulness.

Give a clear reason for your judgement.

**3** Repeat Steps 1 and 2 for **Source C**. Explain how useful the content of **Source C** is for the enquiry topic, then explain how the provenance affects its usefulness for the enquiry topic. Remember to finish with an overall judgement about **Source C**'s usefulness.

**Had a look** ☐  **Nearly there** ☐  **Nailed it!** ☐

# Understanding Question 3b

Question 3b will always be structured in the same way. Make sure you know how this question works and what it is asking you to do.

## How does Question 3b work?

In the exam, Interpretations 1 and 2 will be in the separate Sources and Interpretations Booklet. For this example question, you will find Interpretations 1 and 2 on page 14.

This is the topic for the question. The topic could be anything from your modern depth study and will be the same as the topic in Question 3a.

Identify the command word – this question will always ask you to 'explain'.

**3b Study Interpretations 1 and 2. They give different views about the persecution of minorities in Germany after 1933.**

What is the main difference between these views?

Explain your answer, using details from both interpretations.

**(4 marks)**

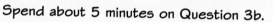

This question will always ask you to identify a difference between the two interpretations.

You need to use details from **both** of the interpretations you are given.

Check how many marks the question is worth – this will help you to manage your time.

## What does Question 3b assess?

✓ Question 3b tests Assessment Objective 4.

✓ You need to show your ability to analyse interpretations.

✓ You will need to identify a key difference between the views in the interpretations and support your explanation with details from the interpretations.

## How long should I spend?

Spend about 5 minutes on Question 3b.

Try not to spend longer than this as Question 3d will need plenty of time.

Take a look at page 17 for more about the assessment objectives.

## Analysing the interpretations

You should:

• focus on the **views** in each interpretation

• look only at the **content** of the interpretations, not at the information about provenance that comes with each one

• in each interpretation, look at the **information** (what is it saying?), **language** and **tone** (how is it saying it?) and **emphasis** (what does it draw attention to?).

## Identifying the main difference

You should:

• focus on the difference in the **views**

• focus on the **overall** message.

For example, the difference could be a difference in attitudes (look for strong words that indicate an opinion, such as triumph or horror), aims, effects, or views about causes or changes.

For example, you could look at whether views are positive or negative, whether change or continuity is emphasised, or whether different causes are emphasised.

**Had a look** ☐ **Nearly there** ☐ **Nailed it!** ☐

# Understanding Question 3b

## What does 'explain' mean?

In Question 3b, **explain** means that you need to use details from the interpretations to support your analysis of the main difference between the views.

> **Remember:** explaining is different to describing. To explain you need to give reasons or evidence.

> For Question 3b, you don't need to consider the provenance of the interpretations – so stay focused on **how** the views differ, not why.

## Supporting your analysis

Use details from the interpretations to back up the main difference you have identified.

You can do this by using a short quotation or by paraphrasing, for example:

> Interpretation 1 says that the Nazis persecuted several groups of people they considered inferior on racial, religious, political or 'health' grounds.

> **Remember:** you must use details from **both** interpretations – you need evidence for the main view you have identified in each.

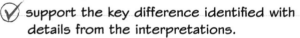

## How is Question 3b marked?

Strong answers to Question 3b:

- ✓ analyse both interpretations
- ✓ identify a key difference of view between the interpretations
- ✓ support the key difference identified with details from the interpretations.

> Remember to use **key terms** in your answer.

## Using language to write clear answers

To make your answer clear, you could introduce your answer like this:

> Interpretation 1...
>
> On the other hand, Interpretation 2....

Turn to page 10 for more about writing clear answers. You can find examples of key terms on page 15.

## Top tips for success

- ✓ Underline any **key words or phrases** in each interpretation as you read them.
- ✓ Identify the **key message** in each interpretation.
- ✓ Look only at the **content** of the interpretations, not at the provenance.
- ✓ Look at the **tone, language and emphasis** of the words the author has chosen to express their ideas.
- ✓ Identify the **main** difference between the viewpoints. There are no extra marks for mentioning more than one.
- ✓ Use **details from each interpretation** to support your answer. This could be a short quotation or paraphrase.
- ✓ Keep your answers **concise** – don't write more than you need to.

**Had a look** ☐ **Nearly there** ☐ **Nailed it!** ☐

# Answering Question 3b

You need to understand how you can write a successful answer to Question 3b.

## Reading the question

> **3b Study Interpretations 1 and 2. They give different views about <u>the persecution of minorities in Germany after 1933</u>.**
>
> What is the main difference between these views?
>
> Explain your answer, using details from both interpretations.
>
> **(4 marks)**

Always read the question carefully before you start writing your answer. Make sure you are clear about what the topic of the question is.

Short, 4-mark questions do not need a plan, but you might find it helpful to underline key points in the interpretations.

## Steps to success

**1** Identify the **key viewpoint** in Interpretation 1.

Interpretation 1 draws attention to the <u>wide range of different groups persecuted by the Nazis</u>.

Identify the **overall** view in the first interpretation.

Make sure your answer relates to the topic in the question.

**2** Add **details** from Interpretation 1 to support what you have said about its viewpoint.

<u>For example, it lists</u> several different minorities that were targeted by the Nazis, including 'Roma and Sinti', 'gay people', 'communists' and 'Jehovah's Witnesses'.

Back up the view you have identified with detail from the interpretation. You can use a short quotation or paraphrase the interpretation.

**3** Identify the **viewpoint** in Interpretation 2 and add **details** from the interpretation to support what you say.

<u>On the other hand, Interpretation 2 emphasises the persecution and murder of the Jews</u>. The treatment of the Jews is described as 'brutal' and it mentions that 30 000 Jews were sent to concentration camps after Kristallnacht.

Identify the overall viewpoint in the second interpretation. This should contrast with the viewpoint you identified in Interpretation 1 – make sure you have identified the main difference between the two interpretations.

Remember to support your point with details from the interpretation.

**Had a look** ☐   **Nearly there** ☐   **Nailed it!** ☐

# Answering Question 3b

## Getting it right

Question 3b should be a good chance to get some straightforward marks. The key for this question is to stay focused on what it is asking you to do – explain the main difference between the views expressed.

> Interpretation 2 focuses on the persecution of the Jews and Interpretation 1 doesn't.

✗ This answer correctly identifies the main difference between the interpretations, but does not provide any supporting detail from them.

> Interpretation 1 emphasises the range of different groups that were persecuted by the Nazis, and Interpretation 2 focuses on one. Interpretation 2 is from the website of the World Holocaust Remembrance Center, so that is why it focuses on the persecution of the Jews.

✗ This answer correctly identifies the main difference. However, instead of providing supporting detail from the interpretations, it discusses provenance, which is not relevant to Question 3b.

> Interpretation 1 is written in a less emotional tone than Interpretation 2, which uses words like 'brutal' and mentions attacks on 'children, elderly and the sick'.

✓ This answer identifies a valid difference – a difference in tone – and uses a quotation from Interpretation 2 to support the point.

✗ However, the difference identified doesn't relate clearly to the question, which asks about the difference in **views**. The answer needs to show how the point about tone relates to the views in the interpretations.

> Interpretation 1 talks about the range of different groups that were persecuted by the Nazis, rather than focusing on one group, as Interpretation 2 does. This might be because Interpretation 2 is looking at one specific example, whereas Interpretation 1 takes an overview of the whole period.

✗ This answer correctly identifies the main difference between the views in the interpretations, but it gives no supporting detail.

✗ This answer then explains why the views might be different, which is not relevant for this question. **Take care:** for Question 3b you need to focus on **how** the views differ, not why.

Compare the examples above with the strong answer on page 65. Remember, a strong answer to Question 3b:
- focuses on the topic in the question
- identifies the main difference between the views in the interpretations
- gives supporting details from each interpretation.

Stay focused on the question and don't write more than you need to.

**Had a look** ☐    **Nearly there** ☐    **Nailed it!** ☐

# Understanding Question 3c

Question 3c will always be structured in the same way. Make sure you know how this question works and what it is asking you to do.

## How does Question 3c work?

Identify the command phrase – this question will always ask you to 'suggest ... why', so you need to explain a reason for the 'different views'.

This tells you that you need to suggest **one** reason.

This is the topic for the question. The topic could be anything from your modern depth study and will be the same as the topic in Questions 3a and 3b.

In the exam, Interpretations 1 and 2 will be in the separate Sources and Interpretations Booklet. For this example question, you will find Interpretations 1 and 2 on page 14.

> **3c** Suggest **one** reason why Interpretations 1 and 2 give different views about the persecution of minorities in Germany after 1933.
>
> You may use Sources B and C to help explain your answer.
>
> **(4 marks)**

In the exam, Sources B and C will be in the separate Sources and Interpretations Booklet. You can use them in your explanation, but you don't have to. For this example question, you will find Sources B and C on page 11.

Check how many marks the question is worth – this will help you to manage your time.

---

## What does Question 3c assess?

- ✓ Question 3c tests Assessment Objective 4.
- ✓ You need to show your ability to analyse interpretations.
- ✓ You will need to explain why the views in the interpretations differ, giving one reason for the difference which is supported by clear evidence from the interpretations.

## How long should I spend?

Spend about 5 minutes on Question 3c.

Try not to spend longer than this as Question 3d will need plenty of time.

Take a look at page 17 for more about the assessment objectives.

---

## What does 'suggest ... why' mean?

You need to give a reason for the difference in the views in the interpretations. Why might the authors be saying different things?

- You need to give only **one** reason, and support it with evidence.
- You should focus on the **content** of the interpretations, **not** on provenance.
- If it is useful, you can refer to Sources B and C to support your explanation.

**Remember:** For Question 3c, it is very important that you **do not** discuss provenance (nature, origin and purpose).

## Questions 3b and 3c

You will already have identified the main difference between the views in your answer to Question 3b. This should help you as you now focus on the **reason** for that difference in Question 3c.

**Had a look** ☐  **Nearly there** ☐  **Nailed it!** ☐

# Understanding Question 3c

## Why might the interpretations differ?

The interpretations might give different views because:

- the authors chose to use different sources
- they have a different emphasis
- they are looking at the subject from different perspectives
- the interpretations given in the exam paper are extracts from longer texts.

## Providing evidence

- You need to support the reason you give in your answer with evidence.
- You should use clear evidence from both of the interpretations.
- You can use the sources to support your explanation – but you don't have to.

Strong answers often make links between the interpretations and the sources.

## How is Question 3c marked?

Strong answers to Question 3c:

- ✓ analyse the interpretations to explain a reason why the views in the interpretations are different
- ✓ support the explanation with evidence from the interpretations and/or the sources.

Remember to use key terms in your answer.

**Top tip**

Turn to page 10 for more about writing clear answers. You can find examples of key terms on page 15.

## Using language to write clear answers

To make your answer clear, start by stating the reason you have identified, like this:

The interpretations give different views about... because...

For each interpretation, make it clear which one you are writing about:

Interpretation 1...

In contrast, Interpretation 2...

## Top tips for success

**Top tip**

- ✓ Quickly read the interpretations and sources again before you start this question. Underline any **key words or phrases** that might help with your answer.
- ✓ Keep your focus on **why** the two interpretations differ.
- ✓ Suggest only **one** reason for the difference between the viewpoints.
- ✓ Back up your suggested reason with clear **evidence** from **both** interpretations.
- ✓ Focus on the **content** of the interpretations, not the provenance.
- ✓ If it can help your explanation, you can refer to Sources B and C in your answer (but you don't have to).
- ✓ Keep your answers **concise** – don't write more than you need to.

**Had a look** ☐    **Nearly there** ☐    **Nailed it!** ☐

# Answering Question 3c

You need to understand how to write a successful answer to Question 3c.

## Reading the question

> **3c** Suggest **one** reason why Interpretations 1 and 2 give different views about the persecution of minorities in Germany after 1933.
>
> You may use Sources B and C to help explain your answer.
>
> **(4 marks)**

Always read the question carefully before you start writing your answer. Make sure you are clear about what the topic of the question is.

Short, 4-mark questions do not need a plan, but you might find it helpful to underline key points in the interpretations, and the sources if you are using them.

## Steps to success

**1** Start by giving **one** possible reason for the interpretations differing. Do this in **one** sentence.

The interpretations give different views about the persecution of minorities in Germany after 1933 because the authors are emphasising different things.

Start by stating one clear reason why you think the interpretations give different views.

**2** Start to explain your reason. Use details from **Interpretation 1**.

Interpretation 1 focuses on the range of minority groups persecuted by the Nazis. Source C supports Interpretation 1, as it shows badges for a range of prisoners targeted by the Nazis.

Back up your reason by referring to Interpretation 1.

If one of the sources supports Interpretation 1, explain how.

**3** Continue your explanation. Use details from **Interpretation 2**.

In contrast, Interpretation 2 is emphasising the impact of Nazi persecution on the Jewish population specifically. This is supported by Source B, which describes the Nazis' plans to target all of Germany's Jews.

Use phrases that help to explain the difference between the views in the interpretations – such as 'In contrast', or 'On the other hand'.

If one of the sources supports the interpretation, explain how.

Keep your answer concise.

**Had a look** ☐  **Nearly there** ☐  **Nailed it!** ☐

# Answering Question 3c

## Getting it right

Question 3c should be another good chance to get some straightforward marks before you attempt the essay question in Question 3d. Stay focused on the question and don't write more than you need to. Look at these examples.

---

The interpretations give different views <u>because they are from different websites</u>. The Holocaust Memorial Day Trust supports Holocaust Memorial Day to remember the victims of the Nazis, while Yad Vashem is a leading centre of education so <u>it's possible that it might have access to more recent information</u>.

✗ This is not a valid reason because it focuses on the origin of the interpretations. Remember that you need to **focus on the content** of the interpretations – not on the provenance (nature, origin, purpose).

✗ This explanation is guessing and is discussing the provenance, which isn't right. You need to back up the reason you give with **evidence from the content of the interpretations**.

---

The interpretations give different views <u>because the historians writing them used different sources</u>. <u>There are hundreds of sources about the persecution of the Jews, and so the sources selected by the two historians led them to write different interpretations.</u>

✓ This is a valid reason.

✗ This explanation is too general. You need to back up your reason with **clear evidence from both interpretations**. You could also use the sources as extra evidence.

---

The interpretations give different views about the persecution of minorities. For example, Interpretation 1 talks about the range of different groups that were persecuted by the Nazis, such as 'Roma and Sinti' and 'communists'. On the other hand, Interpretation 2 emphasises the 'brutal' treatment of Germany's Jewish people in 1938.

✗ This answer explains how the interpretations are different, but for Question 3c you need to write about **why** they are different. Make sure that you stay focused on **why** for this question – **don't** just repeat what you said in your answer to Question 3b!

---

The interpretations give different views about the persecution of minorities in Germany after 1933 <u>because the historians writing them used different sources</u>. <u>Interpretation 1</u> looks at the Nazi persecution of minorities generally, discussing several different groups, and is supported by Source C, which shows badges for a similar range of prisoners. In contrast, Interpretation 2, which considers the increase in Nazi persecution of German Jews after 1938, is supported by the views in <u>Source B</u>.

✓ This is a valid reason.

✓ Clear evidence from both interpretations is used to support the explanation.

✓ The sources are used to support the explanation.

---

**Had a look** ☐    **Nearly there** ☐    **Nailed it!** ☐

# Understanding Question 3d

Question 3d will always be structured in the same way. Make sure you know how this question works and what it is asking you to do.

## How does Question 3d work?

This question will always ask you to 'explain' – you need to give reasons why you agree or disagree with the view in the interpretation.

Identify the command phrase – 'how far' means you need to evaluate the view in the interpretation and make a judgement about whether you agree or disagree with it.

This is the topic for the question. The topic could be anything from your modern depth study and will be the same as the topic in Questions 3a, 3b and 3c.

Check how many marks the question is worth – this will help you to manage your time.

**3d** How far do you agree with Interpretation 1 about the persecution of minorities in Germany after 1933?

Explain your answer, using both interpretations and your knowledge of the historical context.

**(16 marks plus 4 marks for SPaG and use of specialist terminology)**

You **must** analyse and refer to **both** interpretations in your answer.

You **must** use your own knowledge to support your evaluation.

Up to four of the marks of the total for this question will be awarded for good use of spelling, punctuation and grammar, and for use of specialist terminology.

You can find out about SPaG and key terms on pages 16 and 15.

## What does Question 3d assess?

- ✓ Question 3d tests Assessment Objective 4.
- ✓ You need to show your ability to analyse interpretations.
- ✓ You need to show you can evaluate interpretations, make judgements about them and justify your judgements.
- ✓ You need to support your explanation with your knowledge of the historical context.

## How long should I spend?

Spend about 30 minutes on Question 3d.

This question is worth the most marks, so leave enough time to finish your answer.

You don't need to write about both interpretations in the same depth, but you must mention both of them in your answer.

## Understanding the interpretations

- Make sure you understand the view in each interpretation – the interpretations will give contrasting points of view.
- The question will ask you about one interpretation – use the other interpretation to challenge the view it gives.

## Analysing the interpretations

- Consider **how** the view in each interpretation is conveyed – for example, think about the historian's language and tone, what they have emphasised or which details they have chosen to include.
- Look at the interpretations in detail – you need to compare and contrast precise details.

## Questions 3b, 3c and 3d

You will already have explored the differences between views in the interpretations in your answers to Questions 3b and 3c. This should help you as you now focus on evaluating the view in **one** of the interpretations.

**Had a look** ☐    **Nearly there** ☐    **Nailed it!** ☐

# Understanding Question 3d

## 'How far do you agree?'

**You need to reach a judgement** about whether or not you agree with the interpretation in the question.

- Your answer needs to consider the view in the interpretation given in the question, and alternative views, such as the view in the other interpretation.
- Use your knowledge to reach an overall judgement – don't just write down everything you know about the topic.
- Explain why you have made that judgement.

## Your overall judgement

Your overall judgement needs to be supported – you need to include a reason for your decision. In your overall judgement, make sure you:

- say how far you agree with the interpretation – for example, 'Overall, I agree...' or 'Overall, I disagree...'
- give a clear reason for your judgement – say how you have reached this decision, by referring to both interpretations and comparing them to your own knowledge.

## How is Question 3d marked?

Strong answers to Question 3d:

- ✓ give an evaluation which is fully explained
- ✓ consider different views in order to come to a judgement which is supported by reasons
- ✓ support the evaluation with a precise analysis of the interpretations, including how the different views are presented
- ✓ use precisely selected contextual knowledge to support the evaluation
- ✓ give an overall judgement which is supported with reasons
- ✓ present a clear and well-organised argument throughout
- ✓ use correct spelling, punctuation, grammar and specialist terminology.

## Writing analytically

Use phrases that show you are evaluating the viewpoint in the interpretation and making a judgement about that viewpoint. This is called writing analytically. For example:

- I agree/do not agree...
- Although I agree to a certain extent... it is also true that...
- The viewpoint in the interpretation is valid because...
- This view is supported/challenged by...

Remember to use **key terms**.

**Top tip**

You **will** need to write an introduction and conclusion for Question 3d.

## Top tips for success

- ✓ **Plan** your answer to help you to stay focused on the question.
- ✓ Start by stating whether you agree or disagree with the interpretation.
- ✓ Include **arguments that support** the **view** and **counter-arguments**.
- ✓ Use **the other interpretation to challenge** the interpretation in the question.
- ✓ Use **clear and accurate evidence** to support your arguments.
- ✓ Refer to **both interpretations**. You must **examine them both explicitly**.
- ✓ Use **your own information** to support or challenge the interpretation.
- ✓ Give your answer a **clear and logical structure** – for example, PEEL paragraphs.
- ✓ Give an **overall judgement** about how far you agree with the interpretation.

**Top tip**

**Had a look** ☐  **Nearly there** ☐  **Nailed it!** ☐

# Answering Question 3d

You need to understand how to write a successful answer to Question 3d.

## Read the question

Read the question carefully – make sure you are clear about the question topic.

**3d** How far do you agree with Interpretation 1 about the persecution of minorities in Germany after 1933?

Explain your answer, using both interpretations and your knowledge of the historical context.

**(16 marks plus 4 marks for SPaG and use of specialist terminology)**

Make sure you refer to refer to **both** interpretations in your answer.

Check the number of marks. This will help you to use your time well in the exam.

You could use **PEEL** for a clear paragraph structure.
See page 10 for more about PEEL.

## How can I structure my answer?

**1** Write your opening sentence. State clearly whether you agree or disagree with the view in the interpretation the question is asking about.

**2** Begin your argument. You could start by writing about evidence that supports the view in the interpretation.

**3** Continue your argument. If you started with evidence that supports the view in the interpretation, move on to write about evidence that challenges the view in the interpretation.

**4** Write a conclusion. Give an overall judgement about how far you agree with the interpretation and explain why you reached that decision.

## Plan your answer

This question is worth 16 marks (plus 4 marks for SPaG) so take the time to make a good plan.

**Viewpoint in Int 1:** Nazis persecuted wide range of groups; Jews only one of these groups

**Supports Int 1:** early stage – political prisoners; later – persecution of Slavs in occupied territories; 'undesirables' and 'racial purity'

**Challenges Int 1:** details in Int 2; anti-Semitism key for racial purity (e.g. Nuremberg Laws); about 6 million Jews = murdered by the Nazis

**Overall judgement:** Mostly agree with Int 1, but Int 2 more accurate re Jewish persecution

The best answers are structured logically. Include examples of evidence that support and challenge the interpretation.

Include your own knowledge. This detail is not mentioned in the interpretations.

Include notes about both interpretations.

Make a judgement and include it in the plan to help you stay focused.

**Had a look** ☐    **Nearly there** ☐    **Nailed it!** ☐

# Answering Question 3d

## Steps to success

**1** Write your opening sentence. State whether you agree or disagree with the interpretation.

I mostly agree with the view in Interpretation 1 about the Nazi persecution of minorities in Germany after 1933.

Start your answer with a **clear judgement** about the view in the interpretation.

**2** Begin your argument – for example, with evidence that supports the interpretation.

The writer emphasises that a wide range of groups were persecuted by the Nazis after 1933. For example, 'communists' are listed as people who were 'political opponents'. I agree that communists were targeted because I know that in the early stages of the Nazi dictatorship the Nazis sent many political prisoners to concentration camps. …

Show you understand the view in the interpretation.

Consider **how** the view is conveyed. Including short quotations can help you to focus on the detail.

Use your own knowledge to support your points and evaluate the view.

**3** Continue your argument – for example, with evidence that challenges the view in the interpretation.

However, I do not feel that Interpretation 1 gives an accurate picture of the persecution of the Jews. While it is true that many other groups were targeted, the Jews were treated particularly harshly and Interpretation 1 does not mention this. Interpretation 2 challenges the view in Interpretation 1 by describing the 'increased ferocity' of Nazi attacks on Jews and I know that about six million of the people murdered by the Nazis were Jewish. …

Make sure you signpost your counter-argument clearly.

Use phrases that show you are writing analytically and evaluating the views in the interpretations.

Use the other interpretation in your counter-argument.

**4** Write a conclusion. Give an overall judgement about how far you agree with the interpretation.

Overall, I mostly agree with the view in Interpretation 1. The Nazis did target a wide range of minorities and several million political opponents and 'undesirables' were persecuted and murdered. However, I do not think Interpretation 1 gives a clear enough impression of how, overall in Nazi Germany, the Jews were targeted more than other groups. On this point, I think that Interpretation 2 represents the 'ferocity' of the persecution of the Jews more accurately.

Start your conclusion clearly – **give your overall judgement** on the view in the interpretation.

**Explain** your overall judgement by comparing the viewpoints you have considered in your answer.

Refer to both interpretations and your own knowledge.

**Had a look** ☐    **Nearly there** ☐    **Nailed it!** ☐

This is how long you have to answer all the questions for your Paper 3 modern depth study in the exam.

In the exam, Source A is at the beginning of your exam paper booklet and the other sources and interpretations you need are in a separate booklet. Here, you can find Source A on page 44 and the other sources and interpretations on pages 57–58.

Get used to writing with a **black** pen.

In the exam, there will be spaces for you to do this.

For your modern depth study, you need to answer all the questions in both sections of the exam paper.

Focus on answering each question fully, rather than trying to fill all the writing lines.

Use the marks to help you work out how long to spend on each question.

**Pearson Edexcel GCSE (9–1)**

# History
**Paper 3: Modern depth study**
**Option 31: Weimar and Nazi Germany, 1918–39**

**Time:** 1 hour 20 minutes

**You must have:** Sources/Interpretations Booklet

**Instructions**

- Use **black** ink or ball-point pen.
- **Fill in** your name, centre number and candidate number.
- Answer **all** questions in Sections A and B.
- Answer the questions in the spaces provided – there may be more space than you need.

**Information**

- The total mark for this booklet is 52.
- The marks for **each** question are shown in brackets.
- The marks available for spelling, punctuation, grammar and use of specialist terminology are clearly indicated.

In Paper 3, it is Question 3d that has additional marks available for SPaG and use of specialist terminology.

**Top tip**

Make sure you:

- read each question carefully before you start writing your answer
- try to answer every question
- save about five minutes to check your answers at the end.

## SECTION A
### Answer both questions.
### Study Source A below and then answer Question 1.

**Source A:** From a speech given by Adolf Hitler on 17 April 1923. Here, Hitler is giving his views on the armistice and on the Treaty of Versailles.

> With the armistice begins the humiliation of Germany. If the Republic on the day of its foundation had appealed to the country [saying]: Germans, stand together! Up and resist the foe! The Fatherland, the Republic expects of you that you fight to your last breath, then millions who are now enemies of the Republic would be fanatical Republicans. Today they are the foes of the Republic not because it is a Republic but because this Republic was founded at the moment when Germany was humiliated, because it so discredited the new flag that men's eyes must turn regretfully toward the old flag.
>
> So long as this treaty stands there can be no resurrection of the German people; no social reform of any kind is possible! The Treaty was made in order to bring 20 million Germans to their deaths and to ruin the German nation.

Spend **about 5 minutes** on this question.

**Unlocking the question**

You need to **infer** – read between the lines.

**Unlocking the question**

You must make **two** valid inferences.

**Watch out!**

Both your inferences **must** relate to the topic in the question in order to be **valid**.

**Watch out!**

Make sure both your inferences are based on **the content of the source**, not from the information about the provenance.

**Hint**

Make sure your second inference is **different** to your first inference.

**Watch out!**

Make sure your inferences don't just paraphrase the source.

**Hint**

Your supporting details could be a quotation, paraphrase or valid comment on a feature of the source.

---

**1**  Give **two** things you can infer from Source A about Hitler's attitude to the armistice and the Treaty of Versailles.

Complete the table below to explain your answer.

**(4 marks)**

(i) What I can infer:

...................................................................................................

...................................................................................................

...................................................................................................

  Details in the source that tell me this:

...................................................................................................

...................................................................................................

...................................................................................................

(ii) What I can infer:

...................................................................................................

...................................................................................................

...................................................................................................

  Details in the source that tell me this:

...................................................................................................

...................................................................................................

...................................................................................................

**2** Explain why the Nazis were able to establish a dictatorship in Germany in the years 1933–39.

**(12 marks)**

You may use the following in your answer:

- the role of the Gestapo
- censorship and propaganda

You **must** also use information of your own.

......................................................................................................................

......................................................................................................................

......................................................................................................................

......................................................................................................................

......................................................................................................................

......................................................................................................................

......................................................................................................................

......................................................................................................................

......................................................................................................................

......................................................................................................................

......................................................................................................................

......................................................................................................................

......................................................................................................................

......................................................................................................................

......................................................................................................................

......................................................................................................................

......................................................................................................................

......................................................................................................................

......................................................................................................................

......................................................................................................................

......................................................................................................................

......................................................................................................................

......................................................................................................................

......................................................................................................................

......................................................................................................................

......................................................................................................................

......................................................................................................................

......................................................................................................................

......................................................................................................................

......................................................................................................................

**Time**

Spend **about 18 minutes** on this question.

**Top tip**

Always start 12-mark questions with a quick plan. Use the Notes pages at the back of this book if you need extra space – but keep your plan **short**.

**Unlocking the question**

'Explain why' means that you need to give **reasons** for something.

**Watch out!**

Make sure you focus on **explaining why** – don't just describe what happened.

**Unlocking the question**

You need to give **three reasons**. You can use the bullet points in the question if you want to – but you don't have to.

**Watch out!**

Even if you replace the bullet points with your own ideas, you still need **three** reasons overall.

**Revision Guide**

Revise this topic on pages 14–20.

**Hint**

You don't need to write an introduction or a conclusion to your answer for this question.

Unlocking
the question

You **must** include at least
one reason from your own
knowledge.

**Watch out!**

You **don't** have to decide
which reason was more
important.

**LEARN IT!**

Structure your answer
clearly. Use a separate
**PEEL (Point – Evidence –
Explain – Link)** paragraph
to write about each
reason.

**Watch out!**

If there are dates in the
question, your answer
**must** refer to that period.

**Hint**

Clearly **signpost your
reasons** using language
such as 'One reason
was…', 'A second reason
was…'

**Hint**

**Support each reason**
with clear and accurate
information about the
topic in the question.

**Watch out!**

Make sure that you **give
reasons** for the issue in
the question. You need
to say clearly why each
reason you give caused
the consequence in the
question.

.................................................................................

.................................................................................

.................................................................................

.................................................................................

.................................................................................

.................................................................................

.................................................................................

.................................................................................

.................................................................................

.................................................................................

.................................................................................

.................................................................................

.................................................................................

.................................................................................

.................................................................................

.................................................................................

.................................................................................

.................................................................................

.................................................................................

.................................................................................

.................................................................................

.................................................................................

.................................................................................

.................................................................................

.................................................................................

.................................................................................

.................................................................................

.................................................................................

.................................................................................

.................................................................................

.................................................................................

.................................................................................

.................................................................................

.................................................................................

.................................................................................

## LEARN IT!

Use phrases like 'as a result…', 'consequently…' or 'this caused…' to focus your answer and show you are writing analytically.

## Hint

Use **key terms**, like names, dates or specific examples, to support each reason you give.

## Aim higher

Make sure your explanation is analytical and keep it tightly focused on the question **throughout** the answer.

**Time**

Spend **about 12 minutes** on this question.

**Top tip**

For 8-mark questions, make a **short** plan.

**Unlocking the question**

Identify the enquiry topic. You will be focusing on this topic for Questions 3a, 3b, 3c and 3d.

**Unlocking the question**

You need to analyse the **content** and the **provenance** of each source and explain why this makes the source more or less useful.

**Watch out!**

You must refer to **both** sources in your answer.

**Revision Guide**

Revise this topic on pages 10–13.

**Top tip**

Write about one source first, then the other. Finish what you say about each source with an overall judgement about its usefulness.

**Hint**

Analyse the **content** of each source. What does it tell you about the enquiry topic? Is it accurate?

**SECTION B**

**For this section, you will need to use the sources and interpretations on pages 57–58.**

**3a Study Sources B and C.**

How useful are Sources B and C for an enquiry into why support for the Nazis grew in the years 1929–32?

Explain your answer, using Sources B and C and your knowledge of the historical context.

**(8 marks)**

.................................................................................................

.................................................................................................

.................................................................................................

.................................................................................................

.................................................................................................

.................................................................................................

.................................................................................................

.................................................................................................

.................................................................................................

.................................................................................................

.................................................................................................

.................................................................................................

.................................................................................................

.................................................................................................

.................................................................................................

.................................................................................................

.................................................................................................

.................................................................................................

.................................................................................................

.................................................................................................

.................................................................................................

.................................................................................................

.................................................................................................

..................................................................................................................
..................................................................................................................
..................................................................................................................
..................................................................................................................
..................................................................................................................
..................................................................................................................
..................................................................................................................
..................................................................................................................
..................................................................................................................
..................................................................................................................
..................................................................................................................
..................................................................................................................
..................................................................................................................
..................................................................................................................
..................................................................................................................
..................................................................................................................
..................................................................................................................
..................................................................................................................
..................................................................................................................
..................................................................................................................
..................................................................................................................
..................................................................................................................
..................................................................................................................
..................................................................................................................
..................................................................................................................
..................................................................................................................
..................................................................................................................
..................................................................................................................
..................................................................................................................
..................................................................................................................
..................................................................................................................
..................................................................................................................
..................................................................................................................
..................................................................................................................
..................................................................................................................
..................................................................................................................

**Top tip**

Compare the content of each source to your own knowledge. Does it support what you know?

**Unlocking the question**

You **must** use your own knowledge to interpret the sources and support your judgements.

**Hint**

Analyse the **provenance** (nature, origin, purpose) of each source. Does this make the source more or less useful?

**Watch out!**

A source can be useful even if it's unreliable.

**LEARN IT!**

Use phrases like 'quite useful' to give a clear judgement about the usefulness of each source.

**Watch out!**

You should avoid saying a source is useless.

**Hint**

Use key terms to show your topic knowledge.

**Hint**

Stick to any dates given in the question.

**Aim higher**

Evaluate usefulness for the topic of the enquiry **throughout** your answer.

**Time**

Spend **about 5 minutes** on this question.

**Unlocking the question**

You need to identify and explain **one main difference** between the **views** in the interpretations.

**Watch out!**

You need to explain **how** the views differ, not why.

**Unlocking the question**

Use details from **both** interpretations to support your analysis.

**Hint**

Focus on the **overall message** of each interpretation.

**Hint**

For each interpretation, look at the **information, language, tone** and **emphasis**.

**Watch out!**

Look only at the **content** of the interpretations, not the information about provenance.

**Hint**

Support your analysis with short quotations from the interpretations or by paraphrasing them.

**3b** **Study Interpretations 1 and 2. They give different views about why support for the Nazis grew in the years 1929–32.**

What is the main difference between these views?

Explain your answer, using details from both interpretations.

**(4 marks)**

..........................................................................................................

..........................................................................................................

..........................................................................................................

..........................................................................................................

..........................................................................................................

..........................................................................................................

..........................................................................................................

..........................................................................................................

..........................................................................................................

..........................................................................................................

..........................................................................................................

**3c** Suggest **one** reason why Interpretations 1 and 2 give different views about why support for the Nazis grew in the years 1929–32.

You may use Sources B and C to help explain your answer.

**(4 marks)**

..........................................................................................................

..........................................................................................................

..........................................................................................................

..........................................................................................................

..........................................................................................................

..........................................................................................................

..........................................................................................................

..........................................................................................................

..........................................................................................................

..........................................................................................................

..........................................................................................................

..........................................................................................................

### Time

Spend **about 5 minutes** on this question.

### Unlocking the question

You identified the main difference between the views in Question 3b. Now you need to explain **why** the views are different.

### Hint

The views might differ because the authors used different sources, they have a different emphasis or perspective, or because the interpretations are extracts.

### Top tip

State the reason you have identified. Then write about one interpretation, and then the other.

### Hint

Support your reason with clear evidence from **both** the interpretations.

### Watch out!

Look only at the **content** of the interpretations, not the information about provenance.

### Aim higher

Make links between the interpretations and the sources.

## Time

Spend **about 30 minutes** on this question.

## Top tip

Always start 16-mark questions with a good **plan**. Use the Notes pages at the back of this book if you need extra space.

## Revision Guide

Revise this topic on pages 12–13.

## Unlocking the question

'**How far**' means you need to evaluate the view in the interpretation and **make a judgement** about whether you agree or disagree.

## Unlocking the question

The question asks you to **explain**, so you need to give **reasons**.

## Unlocking the question

The interpretations will give contrasting points of view. Make sure you understand the view in each interpretation.

## Top tip

Decide on your judgement before you start writing to help you stay focused.

## Hint

Begin with a clear opening sentence. Say whether you agree or disagree with the interpretation.

**Spelling, punctuation, grammar and use of specialist terminology will be assessed in part 3d.**

**3d** How far do you agree with Interpretation 2 about why support for the Nazis grew in the years 1929–32?

Explain your answer, using both interpretations and your knowledge of the historical context.

**(16 marks plus 4 marks for SPaG and use of specialist terminology)**

.................................................................................................................

.................................................................................................................

.................................................................................................................

.................................................................................................................

.................................................................................................................

.................................................................................................................

.................................................................................................................

.................................................................................................................

.................................................................................................................

.................................................................................................................

.................................................................................................................

.................................................................................................................

.................................................................................................................

.................................................................................................................

.................................................................................................................

.................................................................................................................

.................................................................................................................

.................................................................................................................

.................................................................................................................

.................................................................................................................

.................................................................................................................

.......................................................................

.......................................................................

.......................................................................

.......................................................................

.......................................................................

.......................................................................

.......................................................................

.......................................................................

.......................................................................

.......................................................................

.......................................................................

.......................................................................

.......................................................................

.......................................................................

.......................................................................

.......................................................................

.......................................................................

.......................................................................

.......................................................................

.......................................................................

.......................................................................

.......................................................................

.......................................................................

.......................................................................

.......................................................................

.......................................................................

.......................................................................

.......................................................................

.......................................................................

.......................................................................

.......................................................................

.......................................................................

.......................................................................

.......................................................................

**Unlocking the question**

You explored the differences between the views in the interpretations in Questions 3b and 3c. Now you need to evaluate the view in one of them – whichever is given in the question.

**Hint**

You could start with arguments that support the view in the interpretation given in the question, and then move on to arguments that counter it – or the other way around.

**Unlocking the question**

You need to consider the view in the interpretation given in the question **and** alternative views.

**Top tip**

The question will focus on one interpretation. Use the other one to challenge its viewpoint.

**Hint**

You need to analyse **both** interpretations and refer to **both** of them in your answer.

**Hint**

You **must** support your explanation with your **own knowledge** of the period.

## LEARN IT!

Use phrases like 'on
the other hand' and 'in
contrast' to signpost your
counter-argument.

## Hint

You can get up to four
marks for correct spelling,
punctuation, grammar
and use of specialist
terminology – so leave a
bit of time to check your
writing at the end.

## Aim higher

Consider **how** the views
in the interpretations
are conveyed. Think
about language, tone and
emphasis, and what the
historians have chosen to
include.

## LEARN IT!

Use phrases that show
you are evaluating the
viewpoint and making
a judgement about it –
such as 'I agree/do not
agree...', 'This view is valid
because...' and 'Although I
agree to an extent...'

## Hint

Use key terms to show
your knowledge of the
topic.

## Hint

Include arguments that
support the view in the
interpretation in the
question, as well as
counter-arguments.

..........................................................................................

..........................................................................................

..........................................................................................

..........................................................................................

..........................................................................................

..........................................................................................

..........................................................................................

..........................................................................................

..........................................................................................

..........................................................................................

..........................................................................................

..........................................................................................

..........................................................................................

..........................................................................................

..........................................................................................

..........................................................................................

..........................................................................................

..........................................................................................

..........................................................................................

..........................................................................................

..........................................................................................

..........................................................................................

..........................................................................................

..........................................................................................

..........................................................................................

..........................................................................................

..........................................................................................

..........................................................................................

..........................................................................................

..........................................................................................

..........................................................................................

..........................................................................................

..........................................................................................

**Aim higher**

Compare **precise details** by looking closely at both interpretations.

**Watch out!**

Use your own knowledge to support your analysis and judgement – don't just write down everything you know about the topic.

**Hint**

Structure your answer clearly and logically throughout.

**LEARN IT!**

PEEL (Point – Evidence – Explain – Link) can be a useful way to structure clear paragraphs.

**Aim higher**

Keep an eye on your spelling, punctuation and grammar, and use accurate specialist terminology.

**Hint**

Give an overall judgment and a clear reason for your decision.

**Hint**

You could start your conclusion with 'Overall, I agree/disagree…' or 'In conclusion'.

**Aim higher**

In your conclusion, refer to both interpretations and compare them to your own knowledge.

**Sources for use with Section B.**

**Source B:** From *Germany and the Germans* by Eugen Diesel, published in 1931. Diesel was a German writer and is describing life in Germany after the Great Depression.

> One million seven hundred thousand families are without homes of their own… Thus millions of people exist in conditions of bitter horror, in half-lit dungeons, where six to eight or even fourteen or more human beings are crowded together amid rats and filth. … It sometimes happens that children are born in unheated attics only to die of cold there, and in many slum dwellings the walls drip with damp, and everything gets covered with mould and rot. In thousands of cases one small room and bedroom has to serve as workshop, kitchen, living-room and bedroom for the whole family.

**Source C:** A KPD – Communist Party – propaganda poster from 1932. The figures at the table include Hitler, social democrats and industrialists. The text tells people to vote for the Communist Party (by choosing 'List 3' at the polling station) and calls for 'an end to this system'.

## Interpretations for use with Section B.

**Interpretation 1:** From *Hitler, 1889–1936: Hubris* by Ian Kershaw, published in 1998.

> The loathing and deep fear of Communism that ran through some four-fifths of society was one important common denominator. Faced with a stark choice between National Socialism and Communism – which was how Hitler was increasingly able to portray it after his takeover of power – most middle-class and well-to-do Germans, and even a considerable leaven[1] of the working class, preferred the Nazis. The Communists were revolutionaries, they would take away private property, impose a class dictatorship, and rule in the interests of Moscow. The National Socialists were vulgar and distasteful, but they stood for German interests, they would uphold German values, and they would not take away private property.

[1] **leaven:** number

**Interpretation 2:** From *Hitler, A Study in Tyranny* by Alan Bullock, published in 1952.

> In the six years since … 1923 Germany had made an astonishing recovery. This recovery … was abruptly ended in 1930 under the impact of the [Great] Depression. The fact that 1930 was also the year in which Hitler and the Nazi Party for the first time became a major factor in national politics is not [a coincidence]. Ever since he came out of prison in 1924, Hitler had prophesised disaster, only to see the Republic consolidate[1] itself. … Now, in 1930, disaster cast its shadow over the land again… It was the Depression which tipped the scales against the Republic and for the first time since 1923 shifted the weight of advantage to Hitler's side.

[1] **consolidate:** strengthen

**Hint**

Turn to page 44 to remind yourself about Source A.

**SECTION A**

**Answer both questions.**

1 Give **two** things you can infer from Source A about Hitler's attitude to the armistice and the Treaty of Versailles.

Complete the table below to explain your answer.

**(4 marks)**

First inference is valid inference from source – it is connected to question topic, based on the content of the source, and doesn't just paraphrase the source.

(i) What I can infer:

Hitler was against the armistice. ...............................................

...............................................

...............................................

Details from source support first inference.

Use of short quotation helps to keep supporting detail relevant.

Details in the source that tell me this:

'With the armistice begins the humiliation of Germany.' ...............

...............................................

...............................................

Table spaces used correctly to give clear answer.

Second inference also valid and different from the first one.

(ii) What I can infer:

Hitler thought signing the armistice was a mistake. .....................

...............................................

...............................................

Details from source support second inference.

Answer kept concise.

Details in the source that tell me this:

'men's eyes must turn regretfully toward the old flag' .................

...............................................

...............................................

**Alternative answers**

Answers to Question 1 could also include:
- Hitler thought signing the armistice was a shameful act. **(1)** He says the Republic 'discredited the new flag'. **(1)**
- Hitler thought the terms of the Treaty of Versailles were deliberately very harsh. **(1)** He says the treaty was 'made in order to … ruin the German nation'. **(1)**

2  Explain why the Nazis were able to establish a dictatorship in Germany in the years 1933–39.

(12 marks)

You may use the following in your answer:

- the role of the Gestapo
- censorship and propaganda

You **must** also use information of your own.

**Hint**

Read the notes below, then look at the sample answer that follows.

### Writing a good answer

**Good answers will:**

- give an analytical explanation which is tightly focused on the question throughout
- keep the explanation clear and well-organised throughout
- include information that is accurate, relevant and closely linked to the question
- show a wide range of knowledge and understanding of the topic.

**Relevant points may include:**

- The Gestapo used informants to spy on the German people and identify opponents, so many people lived in fear.
- The Gestapo punished political opponents severely, so people were afraid to speak against the Nazis.
- The Ministry of Enlightenment and Propaganda controlled the press and radio broadcasts so that Germans only heard pro-Nazi ideas.
- The Ministry of Enlightenment and Propaganda organised rallies to promote the Nazi Party, so Germans saw the Nazis as a strong force.
- Hitler introduced projects to reduce unemployment – such as the National Labour Service, the construction of the autobahns and rearmament – so the standard of living improved.

### Q2: sample answer

Plan:

1. Censorship and propaganda
   - Ministry of Enlightenment & Prop. – control of press & radio, rallies
   - Only ideas = Nazi ideas, so Nazis seen as strong

2. Gestapo
   - Spying on citizens, punishing opponents
   - Germans afraid to oppose Nazis

3. Better living standards
   - Before Hitler = unemployment & poverty
   - Nat. Lab. Service, autobahns, rearmament = drop in unemployment by 1939

**Hint**

Look at this sample answer to Question 2. Refer back to the notes above, then look to see how some of the points are used here.

Quick plan helps to keep answer clear and focused.

PEEL (Point – Evidence – Explain – Link) used to give clear structure in every paragraph.

Clear focus on time period given in question.

Relevant and accurate information used as evidence to support point.

Use of key term 'Chancellor' shows strong knowledge of topic.

Each reason clearly signposted, making whole answer well-organised.

Shows accurate and relevant knowledge and understanding of the topic.

Language used shows writing is analytical – shows answer is explaining why.

Answer tightly focused on question throughout.

One reason why the Nazis were able to establish a dictatorship in Germany in the years 1933–39 was their extensive use of censorship and propaganda. The Ministry of Enlightenment and Propaganda was founded soon after Hitler became Chancellor in 1933 and was run by Joseph Goebbels. The Ministry managed the censorship of the press, controlled radio broadcasts and organised mass rallies. As a result, many people from all the different parts of society were surrounded only by ideas that supported the Nazis. Consequently, more and more people were persuaded to see the Nazis as a symbol of strength, and to see Hitler as Germany's saviour, which allowed the Nazi Party to build the dictatorship.

A second reason was the role of the Gestapo. The Gestapo was set up in 1933 by Hermann Goering and was the Nazi's secret police force. They monitored the German population for any signs of opposition and inflicted harsh punishments on political opponents. They also encouraged ordinary German citizens to spy on each other and inform the Gestapo if anyone criticised the Nazi government. This led to an atmosphere of fear, where no one was sure what the Gestapo knew or who might be an informant. As a result, the Nazis were able to establish their dictatorship because it was difficult for anyone to oppose the Nazis and, if they did, they were dealt with by the Gestapo.

A third reason was the improvement in living standards that many Germans experienced after Hitler came to power. Germany had suffered greatly during the First World War and later during the Great Depression of 1929. This had led to an economic crisis, high unemployment and terrible poverty. When he came to power, Hitler tackled these problems through projects such as the National Labour Service, the construction of 7000 km of autobahns and rearmament. As a result, life in Germany started to improve for many, and by 1939 unemployment had fallen to less than half a million. Consequently, many Germans believed Hitler had made their lives better, which meant they were more likely to support him, and this helped the Nazis to create a dictatorship.

Three reasons given overall – including this one from own knowledge.

Key term shows detailed knowledge of the topic.

Explains why the reason caused the consequence in the question.

Specific detail shows wide range of topic knowledge.

Links back to the question.

**A very strong answer because…**

This answer follows a clear, logical structure, with paragraphs beginning 'One reason why...', 'A second reason was....', 'A third reason was...'. This makes the analytical explanation easy to follow. It also means that the answer is tightly focused on the question. The answer provides a good explanation and stays focused on causation – for each point, the student provides relevant and accurate supporting knowledge, then explains how this helped the Nazis establish a dictatorship. The student uses a lot of analytical language, such as 'As a result...', 'This led to...' and 'Consequently...' which shows that they are linking each reason back to the question.

**Hint**

Turn to page 57 to remind yourself about Sources B and C.

**Hint**

Read the notes below, then look at the sample answer on page 64.

**SECTION B**

**3a  Study Sources B and C.**

How useful are Sources B and C for an enquiry into why support for the Nazis grew in the years 1929–32?

Explain your answer, using Sources B and C and your knowledge of the historical context.

**(8 marks)**

**Writing a good answer**

**Good answers will:**

- judge the usefulness of each source for the enquiry given in the question
- explain clearly how the provenance of each source makes it more or less useful
- support their judgements with comments on the content and the provenance of each source
- use own knowledge to interpret the sources and support their judgements.

**Relevant points about Source B may include:**

- The source gives evidence about how difficult living conditions were in Germany after the Great Depression.
- The author was German and lived through the events so can provide a valuable insight.
- The author was a professional writer so may have exaggerated his description for effect.
- The economic collapse led to 5.1 million out of work in September 1932.

**Relevant points about Source C may include:**

- The source shows the communists wanted to take a revolutionary approach.
- It shows the message the Communist Party wanted to give to voters in the 1932 elections.
- It shows the communists intended to completely destroy all aspects of the existing system.
- Large numbers of voters chose to vote for the Nazis rather than the communists in 1932.

**Q3a: sample answer**

**Hint**

Look at this sample answer to Question 3a. Refer back to the notes on page 63, then look to see how some of the points are used here.

Plan:

| Source B | Source C |
|---|---|
| • 'bitter horror' of Great Depression<br>• Unemployment leads to 1932 Nazi election success<br>• Published book by German author<br>• Useful: gives reasons for Nazi support | • Communists to smash system<br>• Fear of revolution and loss of land & businesses<br>• 1932 KPD election poster<br>• Useful: shows communist plans and why people would vote against them |

Quick plan helps to keep answer clear and focused.

Source B is useful for an enquiry into why support for the Nazis grew in the years 1929–32. It describes the 'bitter horror' of life for millions of Germans in 1931, following the Great Depression of 1929. I know that the economic collapse in Germany led to a huge rise in unemployment – from 1.3 million in 1929 to 5.1 million in September 1932. Many became homeless and Source B shows how dreadful the 'slum dwellings' were that they ended up living in. It gives a clear picture of why many voted for the Nazis in the 1932 elections, making them the largest party in the Reichstag, as they thought Hitler was a strong leader who could improve their lives. Source B is probably reliable evidence of what life in Germany was like after the Depression because the author is German and the book was published in 1931 – so he was living through it. However, as a writer, he might have wanted to draw attention to the suffering to try to get politicians to improve living conditions. So it is possible that he is exaggerating the situation for effect. However, it is still useful because it shows the impact of the Great Depression, which suggests why people may have supported the Nazis.

Answer looks at one source at a time, giving clear structure.

Begins with clear judgement about first source.

Analyses content of first source, staying focused on enquiry topic.

Compares source content to own knowledge.

Short quotations used to support points.

Analyses provenance of first source and explains effect on usefulness.

Finishes analysis of first source with overall judgement about its usefulness.

Content and provenance of second source analysed.

Language used shows focus on giving clear judgement.

Uses own knowledge to explain how source content fits with enquiry topic.

Use of key terms shows strong knowledge of topic.

Considers accuracy of source and how this affects usefulness.

Gives clear reason for overall judgement about second source.

Source C is also useful for this enquiry. It shows an aggressive-looking communist who wants 'an end to this system'. We know that the communists were opposed to democracy and, for example, in 1919 the Spartacists had tried to set up a communist government in Berlin. Source C shows how determined the KPD were to introduce a completely new way of running the country, as the figure is about to smash up the Weimar government, industrialists and businessmen and Hitler, who are all sitting at the table. This suggests why the middle and upper classes in particular supported the Nazis at this time, as they feared communists would take their land and businesses. Source C is a Communist Party propaganda poster for the 1932 elections. It is reliable because it clearly shows the message the KPD wanted to give to voters – that they intended to take a revolutionary approach. It also shows that the communists considered all existing political parties and businesses as part of the system they wanted to get rid of. Therefore, this is a useful source for the enquiry as it gives a reason why the other parties, including the Nazi Party, opposed the communists, as well as why large numbers of Germans would have looked to the Nazis instead.

**A very strong answer because...**

This answer examines both sources and makes a clear judgement about the usefulness of each one. The student analyses the content of each interpretation, comparing it to their own knowledge. The student also considers the provenance of each source and explains how this affects its usefulness. Throughout the answer, the student uses relevant examples from the sources to support their points. They also use their own knowledge to interpret the sources and to support their judgement about each one. The structure is clear, with one source analysed first and then the other. Starting with a quick plan has helped the student to keep their answer tightly focused on the question throughout.

**3b Study Interpretations 1 and 2. They give different views about why support for the Nazis grew in the years 1929–32.**

What is the main difference between these views?

Explain your answer, using details from both interpretations.

**(4 marks)**

**Hint**

Turn to page 58 to remind yourself about Interpretations 1 and 2.

**Hint**

Read the notes below, then look at the sample answer that follows.

**Writing a good answer**

**Good answers will:**

- analyse both interpretations
- identify a key difference of view between the interpretations
- support the key difference identified with details from the interpretations.

**Relevant points may include:**

- A main difference is that Interpretation 1 focuses on how Germans' fear of communism led to growth in support for the Nazis, while Interpretation 2 emphasises the role of the Great Depression and how the Germans looked to the Nazis for a solution.

**Q3b: sample answer**

Interpretation 1 says that support for the Nazis grew because people were afraid of communism. For example, it says most Germans had a 'deep fear' of communists who they thought would 'rule in the interests of Moscow', so they 'preferred the Nazis'.

On the other hand, Interpretation 2 says that support for the Nazis grew because of the Great Depression. It describes how the Depression 'cast its shadow' over Germany and says this gave the Nazis and Hitler an advantage.

Clear structure helps to keep answer concise.

Main difference between the viewpoints clearly identified.

**Hint**

Look at this sample answer to Q3b. Refer back to the notes above, then look to see how some of the points are used here.

Both interpretations analysed.

Answer stays focused on the content of the interpretations.

Details from interpretations used to back up main viewpoints identified and to keep focused on how the viewpoints differ.

**A very strong answer because...**

This answer is concise and tightly focused on the overall message in each interpretation. The student clearly identifies the main difference between the views in the interpretations, and both interpretations are analysed in the answer. The focus is correctly on the content of the interpretations, rather than provenance, and the student supports their explanation with details from both interpretations. Use of quotations and paraphrasing helps keep the answer focused on how the views in the interpretations are different.

## Hint

Turn to pages 57 and
58 to remind yourself
of Sources B and C and
Interpretations 1 and 2.

## Hint

Read the notes below,
then look at the sample
answer that follows.

**3c** Suggest **one** reason why Interpretations 1 and 2 give different views about
why support for the Nazis grew in the years 1929–32.

You may use Sources B and C to help explain your answer.

(4 marks)

### Writing a good answer

**Good answers will:**

• analyse the interpretations to explain a reason why the views in the interpretations are different

• support the explanation with evidence from the interpretations and/or the sources.

**Relevant points may include:**

• The interpretations may differ because they have given weight to different sources. For example, Source C
provides some support for Interpretation 1, which focuses on the fear of communism. Source B provides some
support for Interpretation 2, which emphasises the impact of the Great Depression.

• They may differ because the authors have a different emphasis. Interpretation 1 is dealing with how a fear of
communism led Germans to support the Nazis. Interpretation 2 is dealing with how people looked to the Nazis
to solve the economic problems after the Great Depression.

• They may differ because they are written from different perspectives. Interpretation 1 looks at the political situation
and the threat of communism. Interpretation 2 focuses on the economic situation after the Great Depression.

## Hint

Look at this sample answer
to Q3c. Refer back to the
notes above, then look
to see how some of the
points are used here.

One reason for the different
views is clearly stated at the
beginning of the answer.

Gives evidence from content
of interpretations, keeping
focus on why they differ.

Sources used to support
explanation.

Gives evidence from both
interpretations.

### Q3c: sample answer

The interpretations give different views about why support for the
Nazis grew in the years 1929–32 because the authors have given
weight to different sources. Interpretation 1 focuses on the fear most
Germans had of the Communist Party and its revolutionary ideas.
The author might have been influenced by Source C, which depicts a
communist who is about to destroy the other parties and the system.
Interpretation 2 focuses on the disastrous effects of the Great
Depression in Germany. This reflects the description of the terrible
poverty affecting millions of Germans in Source B, so the author of
Interpretation 2 may have given weight to Source B.

### A very strong answer because...

This concise answer gives one reason why the views are different, supported with clear evidence from the
content of both interpretations. The answer stays focused on why the views differ and the sources are used to
support the explanation. The student does not just repeat their answer to Question 3b.

Spelling, punctuation, grammar and use of specialist terminology will be assessed in part 3d.

**Hint**

Turn to page 58 to remind yourself about Interpretations 1 and 2.

**3d** How far do you agree with Interpretation 2 about why support for the Nazis grew in the years 1929–32?

Explain your answer, using both interpretations and your knowledge of the historical context.

**(16 marks plus 4 marks for SPaG and use of specialist terminology)**

**Hint**

Read the notes below, then look at the sample answer on page 69.

**Writing a good answer**

Good answers will:

- give an evaluation which is fully explained
- consider different views in order to come to a judgement which is supported by reasons
- support the evaluation with a precise analysis of the interpretations, including how the different views are presented
- use precisely selected contextual knowledge to support the evaluation
- give an overall judgement which is supported with reasons
- present a clear and well-organised argument throughout
- use correct spelling, punctuation, grammar and specialist terminology.

**Relevant points from the provided material and own knowledge which support this may include:**

- Interpretation 2 links the collapse of the German economy in 1930 to the Great Depression.
- Interpretation 2 suggests that the economic crisis gave the Nazi Party an advantage over the Weimar Republic.
- Unemployment rose swiftly after the Great Depression, leaving millions of Germans homeless and in poverty.
- The Nazis used the strength of Hitler's personality and propaganda to convince Germans that they would rescue the country from the crisis.

**Relevant points from the provided material and own knowledge which challenge this may include:**

- Interpretation 1 suggests that the majority of Germans were afraid of communism.
- Interpretation 1 suggests that if the communists came to power they would revolutionise the way Germany was run and would act against German interests.
- Middle- and upper-class Germans were particularly worried about communism, afraid that they would lose their property and businesses.
- In the July 1932 elections the communists won 15% of votes compared to the Nazis' 38%.

**Hint**

Look at this sample answer
to Q3d. Refer back to the
notes on page 68, then
look to see how some of
the points are used here.

Good plan helps to keep
answer clear and focused.

Starts with a clear judgement
about the view in the
interpretation the question
asks about.

Shows understanding of the
view in the interpretation.

View in interpretation
analysed in detail.

Accurate spelling of 'Weimar'.

Language used shows writing
is analytical.

Use of key terms shows
strong knowledge of the
topic.

Short quotations used to
focus on the detail.

Good use of specialist
terminology in the phrase
'share prices crashed'.

Clear and accurate evidence
used to support argument.

**Q3d: sample answer**

Plan:

| Viewpoint in Int 2 – Support for Nazis grew because of effects of Great Depression | |
| --- | --- |
| Supports Int 2: | • Depression – economic collapse<br>• Unemployment, poverty, homelessness<br>• Nazis = party to rescue Germany |
| Challenges Int 2: | • Int 2 – fear of communism<br>• Int 2 – communism = revolutionary<br>• Int 2 – Nazis preferred over communists |
| Overall judgement | Mainly agree with Int 2 but Int 1 also right as people were afraid of communism |

I mainly agree with the view in Interpretation 2 about why support for
the Nazis grew in the years 1929–32. Interpretation 2 emphasises
economic factors. The author uses the word 'astonishing' to describe
the recovery after the hyperinflation of 1923, which suggests the
recovery was surprising given the weaknesses of the Weimar government
and helps to underline how bad things had been in the early 1920s.
He goes on to say that the Depression ended the recovery 'abruptly'
which emphasises how fragile the recovery was as well as the brutal
impact of the Depression. This viewpoint is valid because I know that
the Wall Street Crash of October 1929 was devastating for the
German economy. It caused the USA to withdraw money from German
industry. In the summer of 1931 the German economy collapsed, and by
September 4.3 million Germans were unemployed.

Interpretation 2 twice describes the Depression as a 'disaster' and
I agree that the consequences were catastrophic. Many Germans
had lost their savings when share prices crashed in 1929. The
German government increased taxes and cut unemployment benefits,
and employers cut wages. These factors, together with rocketing
unemployment, meant that many found themselves homeless and
suffering terrible poverty.

Clear paragraphs keep argument well-organised throughout.

Interpretation 2 links this economic crisis with the growth in Nazi support, saying that it was 'not [a coincidence]' that Germans turned to Hitler at this time. I agree with this assessment as it is true that the Nazis did use the opportunity to present themselves as the party that would rescue Germany from what they believed to be the failures of the Weimar Republic. Hitler presented himself as a strong leader and used propaganda to convince a wide range of Germans – including businessmen, the working class, farmers and women – that he would not only solve the economic problems, but also restore law and order. As a result, Hitler had 'the weight of advantage' and in the July 1932 elections the Nazis became the largest party in the Reichstag, with 230 seats.

However, the Depression was not the only reason that support for the Nazis grew and Interpretation 1 is right to challenge the viewpoint in Interpretation 2 by emphasising the Germans' 'loathing and deep fear' of communism. Many working-class people supported the communists because they felt the KPD would protect their jobs, and the KPD did increase their percentage of the vote from 10% in 1928 to 15% in 1932. However, most middle- and upper-class Germans were afraid a communist government would, as Interpretation 1 says, 'take away private property' and 'rule in the interests of Moscow'.

Links argument back to the question.

Use of key terms shows strong knowledge of the topic.

Beginning of counter-argument clearly signposted.

Alternative views considered.

Analyses and refers to both interpretations.

Focuses on how the view in the interpretation is conveyed here, by looking at choice of details.

Selects precise details from knowledge of historical context to support argument.

Other interpretation used to support counter-argument.

Accurate spelling, punctuation, grammar and use of specialist terminology throughout.

Own knowledge used to support point.

Own knowledge used to evaluate interpretation.

Considers other interpretation in detail.

Interpretation 1 describes the communists as 'revolutionaries' and this is right, as the aim of the communists was to completely change the way Germany was governed. Interpretation 1 claims that 'four-fifths of society' was afraid of communism and it is true that the fear was widespread. Many people remembered the violent Spartacist Revolt of 1919, and there was regular fighting between the communists and the Nazis before elections in 1932. The author contrasts the communists with the Nazis, suggesting that even though people thought the Nazis were 'vulgar and distasteful', at least they 'stood for German interests', so Germans 'preferred' them. This is supported by the July 1932 election results where the communists won 15% of votes compared to the Nazis' 38%.

Ends with conclusion that gives clear overall judgement.

Overall judgement fully supported and explained with clear reason.

Overall judgement refers to both interpretations and compares them to own knowledge.

Overall, I mainly agree with the view in Interpretation 2. The Nazis exploited the economic collapse that followed the Great Depression to present themselves as Germany's saviours from 'disaster'. However, Interpretation 1 correctly describes the 'stark choice' between the Nazis and communists in this period, showing that, as many feared a communist revolution, support for the Nazis increased.

Links judgement back to question focus.

**A very strong answer because...**

This answer analyses both interpretations, and the student comes to a clear judgement about whether or not they agree with the interpretation given in the question. The student considers how the view in each interpretation is conveyed and uses precise evidence from each one to support their points, before linking back to the question. This keeps the answer tightly focused on analysis. The argument is also supported with relevant information from the student's own knowledge of the topic. The counter-argument is clearly signposted, and the student reaches an overall judgement in the conclusion which is explained. Starting with a good plan has helped the student to organise their argument clearly and to stay focused on the question. Spelling, punctuation, grammar and use of specialist terminology are also accurate throughout.

# Answers

*Where an exemplar answer is given, this is not necessarily the only correct response. In most cases there is a range of responses that can gain full marks.*

## KNOWLEDGE BOOSTER

## 1. The Weimar Republic, 1918–29

1 A

2

| Strengths of the Weimar constitution | Weaknesses of the Weimar constitution |
|---|---|
| • Proportional representation meant small parties were represented.<br><br>Plus any one from:<br>• Women had the vote.<br>• No one group or person could get too much power.<br>• Presidential elections held every 7 years. Local government had some control over the regions.<br>• Reichsrat could regulate the power of the Reichstag by delaying new laws. | • Proportional representation often led to weak coalition governments.<br><br>Plus any one from:<br>• Lack of strong government led to weakness during crisis.<br>• It was not what the people wanted so did not have public support. |

3 For example, any two from:
   • People were angry that their leaders had accepted responsibility for the war.
   • The reparations agreed by the government weakened the economy.
   • Germany had lost 13% per cent of its territory in Europe, which made the country weaker and damaged the economy.
   • It also lost 11 overseas colonies, which made the country less prestigious.
   • People were angry that the government agreed to demilitarisation.
   • The army felt that the government had 'stabbed them in the back'.

4 Spartacists A, D, F; Freikorps B, C, E

5 Reparations payments damaged the German <u>economy</u>. In 1922, the Weimar government could not pay reparations and asked for more time. In <u>January 1923</u>, France invaded the <u>Ruhr</u> to take goods and raw materials instead. German workers went on <u>strike</u>. This was a disaster for the economy. The government <u>printed</u> more money to try to solve the problem but the value of the mark kept dropping until it became worthless. This is called <u>hyperinflation</u>.

## 2. The Weimar Republic, 1918–29

6 • Stresemann sets up the Rentenmark, more secure, ends hyperinflation.
   • Dawes Plan, 1924, <u>reparations payments reduced, US banks lent money to German businesses</u>.
   • Young Plan, <u>reduced reparations further and gave Germany longer to pay, government could reduce taxes</u>.
   • Secure currency and US loans gave Germany longer to pay, government could reduce taxes, increase confidence, economy improves.

7 Aii; Biii; Ci

8 Any one from:
   • Strengthened German people's confidence in their government
   • Increased support for moderate political parties
   • Foreign loans meant lower taxes
   • Businesses could borrow money needed to expand
   • French withdrawal from Rhineland boosted the economy

9 A. False – the housing shortage continued, although there was some improvement; B. True; C. False – most women gave up work when they married; D. True; E. False – exciting new films challenged traditional cinema; F. True

## 3. Hitler's Rise, 1919–33

1 (a) He was angry about the way Germany was treated in the Treaty of Versailles.
   (b) The Twenty-Five Point Programme
   (c) 1921

2 The Sturmabteilung, or SA, were an armed group who provided protection for Nazi rallies and disrupted the meetings of opposing parties.

3 B and C (The other two were short-term causes.)

4

| Negative consequences | Positive consequences |
|---|---|
| Hitler was sent to prison.<br><br>Plus any one from:<br>• The NSDAP was banned<br>• The putsch failed, which was humiliating | While he was in prison, he wrote *Mein Kampf*, which spread his ideas.<br><br>Plus any one from:<br>• He used his trial to publicise his views<br>• The putsch made Hitler realise that he needed to rethink his tactics |

5 Any two from:
   • Hitler writes Mein Kampf, which makes his key ideas clear.
   • Hitler is released from prison.
   • The ban on the NSDAP is lifted in 1925.
   • The failure of the Munich Putsch makes Hitler realise that violence and force aren't enough to win national support.

6 The Bamberg Conference of 1926.

## 4. Hitler's rise, 1919–33

7 • After 1929 Wall Street Crash, USA stopped lending money to Germany and demanded all loans repaid.
   • Government had no money, so <u>raised taxes, cut benefits and cut jobs.</u>
   • Businesses had to <u>pay higher taxes and pay back loans, so had far less money.</u>
   • Millions of job losses meant that <u>poverty was widespread.</u>
   • Impact of unemployment: support for Nazis and communists increases.

8 Any two from:
   • Hitler was a powerful speaker and a strong leader.
   • The SA disrupted the activities of opposition parties.
   • Nazi propaganda targeted every section of the German population.
   • People were frightened of communism and the Nazis promised to oppose it.
   • The depression made people unhappy with the government and support for extreme parties grew.

9 A3; B1; C2; D7; E4; F6; G5

## 5. Nazi dictatorship, 1933–39

1 The communists

2 A, B and D. (The constitution was not scrapped (C) but Hitler could pass laws that overruled it.)

3 A4; B2; C5; D1; E3

4

| SS (Nazi Party protection squad) | SD (Security service) | Gestapo (Secret police) |
|---|---|---|
| • Led by Himmler<br><br>Plus any two from:<br>• Controlled all police and security forces<br>• Ran the concentration camps<br>• Wore uniforms | • Led by Heydrich<br><br>Plus any two from:<br>• Spied on opponents of the Nazi Party at home and abroad<br>• Wore uniforms | • Set up by Goering, led by Heydrich<br><br>Plus any two from:<br>• Sent people to concentration camps<br>• Spied on people at home<br>• Prosecuted people for speaking out against Nazis<br>• Wore plain clothes |

5 Any one from:
   • Hitler abolished trial by jury – verdicts were decided by Nazi-controlled judges.
   • In cases of treason, trials took place in secret and Hitler chose the judges.

   • Judges had to belong to the National Socialist League for the Maintenance of the Law, which brought them under Nazi control.
   • Judges had to favour the Nazi Party in their decisions.

6 A. True; B. True; C. False – it was one of Hitler's main opponents; D. True; E. False – once Hitler had increased his power, he broke the agreement to allow Catholics to worship and run their own schools.

## 6. Nazi dictatorship, 1933–39

7 a) In 1933
   b) To monitor all aspects of culture and make sure they were consistent with Nazi ideas
   c) Goebbels

8 Once Hitler took power in <u>1934</u>, most Germans <u>accepted</u> Nazi leadership. One reason for this was that the Nazis reduced <u>unemployment</u> and Hitler's <u>foreign</u> policy was successful. Another reason was that censorship and <u>propaganda</u> meant people only heard <u>positive</u> messages about the Nazis. It also meant that many people who were <u>opposed</u> to the Nazis were afraid to speak out, although several groups opposed the Nazis in secret.

9 A. True; B. True; C. False – he voted for the party in 1933, but went on to become one of the Nazis' main church opponents; D. True

10 A, B and D

## 7. Nazi Germany, 1933–39

1

| The Nazis believed that a woman should: | They believed that a woman should not: |
|---|---|
| • Stay at home with their family<br>Plus any two from:<br>• Look after the home<br>• Wear traditional clothes<br>• Have lots of children | • Go out to work<br><br>Plus any two from:<br>• Wear makeup<br>• Drink alcohol<br>• Go to university |

2 Ai and ii; Bi; Ci and iii

3 A. True (from 1939); B. False – it was for girls aged 14–18; C. True; D. True; E. False – they were for girls as well as boys.

4 All are correct

5 Any two from:
   • PE was emphasised to ensure a healthy and strong population.
   • Girls were taught domestic skills, while boys were taught science and military skills.
   • Both sexes were taught the traditional subjects of German, History, Geography and Maths.
   • Race Studies and Eugenics were taught to both sexes.

**6** Any one from:
- Nazi posters and flags in classrooms.
- Only approved textbooks containing Nazi ideas.
- Racial ideas and anti-Semitism were embedded in subjects.
- Lessons began and ended with the Nazi salute.

## 8. Nazi Germany, 1933–39

**7** Any two from:
- National Labour Service
- Building sports facilities, for example for the Berlin Olympics
- Constructing 7000km of autobahns
- Rearmament
- New public buildings

**8** Aii; Biii; Ci

**9** Hitler believed that the Aryan race was destined to be a 'master race'. Non-Aryans (Roma and Sinti people, Slavs, black people and Jews) were seen as 'Untermenschen' or subhumans. Hitler wanted to increase the number of 'pure' Germans, so Aryans were expected to marry other Aryans. Other groups were called 'undesirable' – homosexuals were imprisoned and mentally handicapped people were sterilised.

**10** Any two from the following. Jewish people:
- could be German subjects but not citizens
- could not vote or work for the government
- had to wear a yellow star-shaped patch sewn on their clothes for ease of identification
- could not marry a German citizen
- could not have a sexual relationship with a German citizen.

**11** Uniformed and non-uniformed gangs attacked Jewish communities, destroying homes, shops, businesses and synagogues.

# Notes

# Notes

# Notes